HOW TO READ THE BIBLE
(as if your life depends on it)

HOW
TO READ THE
BIBLE
(as if your life depends on it)

MICHAEL YOUSSEF

SALEM
BOOKS
an imprint of Regnery Publishing
Washington, D.C.

Published in association with the literary agency of THE GATES GROUP.
Salem Books™ is a trademark of Salem Communications Holding Corporation.
Regnery® and its colophon are registered trademarks of Salem Communications Holding Corporation.

Cataloging-in-Publication data on file with the Library of Congress.

ISBN: 978-1-68451-505-9
eISBN: 978-1-68451-511-0

Published in the United States by
Salem Books
An Imprint of Regnery Publishing
A Division of Salem Media Group
Washington, D.C.
www.SalemBooks.com

Manufactured in the United States of America

10 9 8 7 6 5 4 3

Books are available in quantity for promotional or premium use.
For information on discounts and terms, please visit our website:
www.SalemBooks.com

I dedicate this book in memory of D. W. B. Robinson,
the former Archbishop of Sydney, who taught me the necessity
of understanding the Bible, both Old and New Testaments,
as a unified whole.

"By faith, he still speaks, even though he is dead."
Hebrews 11:4

CONTENTS

PART VI: THE BOOK THAT HEALS

Sixty-Six Books, One Story

We sometimes hear that Christians should defend the Bible against attacks from unbelievers. This is a well-intentioned notion, but as Martin Luther pointed out, defending the Bible is like defending a lion. A lion doesn't need us to defend it, and neither does God's Word. Any attempt on our part to defend the Bible would be pointless. We are hopelessly inadequate to the task.

Down through the centuries, philosophers have tried to destroy the Bible by argument and criticism. Dictators have tried to destroy it by force. Governments have passed laws to suppress and forbid it. Yet the Word of God still stands.

I pray that the Holy Spirit, the Author of the Bible, would take these poor words of mine and use them to spark a revival in our lives, for revival can begin only in the life of a Christian who feeds daily on the Word of God. If we read and heed the Bible—if we take hold of its mighty power, if we live in it, apply it, and obey it—the Holy Spirit will move in our lives and revive our deadened spirits.

Gideons International is a Christian association known for placing Bibles in hotel and motel rooms, hospitals, colleges, military bases, and prisons. All those Bibles have an introduction that includes these words:

> The Bible contains the mind of God, the state of man, the way of salvation, the doom of sinners, and the happiness of believers...Read it to be wise, believe it to be safe, and practice it to be holy...It is the traveler's map, the pilgrim's staff, the pilot's compass, the soldier's sword, and the Christian's charter.... Read it slowly, frequently, and prayerfully.[1]

These are wise words. There is no other book like the Bible. God used at least forty different human writers over a period of more than 1,600 years to write the sixty-six books of the Old and New Testaments. The writers of the Bible range from kings to shepherds, from a physician to a tax collector. It was composed on three different continents: Europe, Asia, and Africa.

Yet the Bible is truly a single Book with a single Author, focused on a single theme—and that theme is Jesus Christ the Redeemer. It's the story of the Kingdom of God and its King. The books of the Old Testament tell us that He is coming. The books of the New Testament announce He has arrived. The Old Testament anticipates Jesus. The New Testament proclaims Him gladly. And passages in both the Old and New Testaments promise that He is coming again in all His might and majesty.

The unity of the Bible confounds human wisdom, baffles its critics, and challenges its enemies. There is no book like this Book because there is no author like its Author.

The sixty-six books of the Bible do not tell sixty-six stories; together, they tell one story. It is the story of humanity's rebellion against God and God's redemptive love for the human race—a love expressed in salvation for all who repent of their rebellion and sin. It's the story of a Kingdom and a Covenant, and one Lord who rules eternally.

Come with me on an adventure. Let's explore the Book together and learn to love it as if our lives depend on it.

Because they do.

PART I

The Unity of God's Word

At least forty human writers wrote the sixty-six books of the Old and New Testaments across a span of sixteen centuries, yet it is one book telling one story about one Person, Jesus the Messiah, and one Kingdom, the Kingdom of God. There is no more tested book than the Bible. It has been scrutinized up, down, and sideways, examined critically by countless authorities through the years—yet there it stands.

1

The Life-Changing Book

In May 1967, Egypt expelled United Nations peacekeepers from the Sinai Peninsula and closed the Straits of Tiran to Israeli ships, blockading Israel from the Red Sea—a precursor to war. Egypt, Jordan, Syria, and Lebanon mobilized their armies and moved to encircle Israel. The leaders of those nations spoke openly of erasing Israel from the map.

On June 4, Israeli Defense Minister Moshe Dayan gathered his senior officers, who thought they were being summoned to a council of war. Dayan surprised them by taking out a Bible and opening it to 1 Samuel 17. Without explanation, he began reading to them the account of David and Goliath.

David, a young Hebrew shepherd boy, had defeated a strong, heavily armored Philistine soldier by attacking the enemy's weak points. David knew Goliath's heavy armor would slow him down. Despite his armor, Goliath had a vulnerable spot—his unprotected face. So David whirled his sling at the exposed target. The stone struck Goliath in the forehead, and he fell dead.

The officers shifted uncomfortably in their chairs. Israel was surrounded by enemies and facing annihilation. What was the point of this ancient story from the distant past?

Dayan closed the Bible and told his officers that the story of David and Goliath had inspired a plan. Like Goliath, Israel's modern-day enemies had a vulnerable spot—and that was where Israel would strike.

At 7:10 the next morning, June 5, Israeli fighter jets launched a raid on Egyptian airfields. Within hours, the Egyptian air force was destroyed.

After just 132 hours of fighting—later known as the Six-Day War—the tiny nation of Israel had defeated the combined armed forces of Egypt, Jordan, and Syria. When the dust settled, Israel controlled the Sinai and Gaza Strip (captured from Egypt), the West Bank and East Jerusalem (captured from Jordan), and the Golan Heights (captured from Syria), enlarging Israel's territory by an additional 26,000 square miles.

Historians agree that the war was really decided in those first few hours when the Israeli air force struck the enemy's most vulnerable point and achieved command of the skies. And the plan for victory was inspired by an ancient story from the Bible.

The Word of God is as relevant today as it was when the ink was still wet on its parchment. The same ancient, divinely inspired wisdom that inspired Israel to fight and win is still ready to inspire you and me to live the victorious Christian life. We need to read and understand God's Word as if our lives depend on it. Once we truly understand the Bible, it will become our sword and shield. It will show us how to defeat our spiritual enemy, Satan, so that we can take territory for Christ and His Kingdom.

The Least-Read Bestseller

The Bible is truly a life-changing Book because its Author is a life-changing God. Throughout history, people have either loved the Word of God or hated it. People have either believed it or rejected it. They have tried to change it, they have tried to edit out the parts that offended them, they have tried to water down its message. Dictators and despots have sought to burn or banish the Bible—yet they are dead, and God's Word lives.

Year after year, the Bible is the bestselling book in the world—yet most Bibles end up on a shelf, gathering dust. According to the American Bible Society and the Barna Group, just 18 percent of American adults spend any time reading the Bible.[1] This means that 82 percent of adults allow their Bibles to sit unopened and unused, making the Bible the least-read bestseller of all time. This is undoubtedly one of the chief reasons for the moral and spiritual decline in our culture.

Why do so many Christians claim to love God while ignoring His Word? Why do so many Christians who claim to love Jesus spend hours with their eyes glued to TikTok, Instagram, or Netflix—yet have no time for God's Word? Again and again, I hear people say, "I would love to read the Bible, but there's just not enough time in my day." If you have ever said similar words, then honestly examine your life and your priorities. Ask yourself, "Am I being honest with myself—and with God? Can I say I truly love Jesus if I neglect God's Word?"

After more than half a century of walking with the Lord, I can confidently say that the Bible is the only spiritual food that will nourish your soul. Daily reading of the Word of God is the only power for living. It's the only mirror that will reveal the truth about the real you. And it's the only washing and cleansing agent that can truly purify you.

Let's look at each of these four dimensions of God's Word.

1. Our Only Spiritual Food

I believe in preaching God's Word from the pulpit. I believe in the validity and power of teaching God's Word in Sunday school classes, in Christian books, and on Christian radio and television broadcasts and internet sites. I preach and teach God's Word through every one of those mediums.

But I must say, on the authority of God's Word, that the Bible itself is the only food that will spiritually nourish and sustain you, and is the only food that will spiritually encourage you to grow stronger every day.

The Scriptures often draw an analogy between the physical body and the spiritual body, and between physical food and the spiritual food of the Bible. Just as our physical body needs nutritious food in order to be strong, so our spiritual health depends on spiritual food.

In Deuteronomy 8:3, Moses said to the people of Israel,

> He humbled you, causing you to hunger and then feeding you with manna, which neither you nor your ancestors had known, to teach you that man does not live on bread alone but on every word that comes from the mouth of the LORD.

These are the very words from the Old Testament that Jesus quoted in order to defeat Satan in the wilderness: "It is written: 'Man shall not live on bread alone, but on every word that comes from the mouth of God'" (Matthew 4:4; see also Luke 4:4).

And Job, that faithful saint, said, "I have not departed from the commands of His lips; I have treasured the words of His mouth more than my daily bread" (Job 23:12).

Few Americans have had to miss many meals. I'm not saying we should feel guilty for living in a land of plenty. Rather, we should feel grateful to God while keeping the mindset of Job. We should treasure the Word of God more than our daily bread. How can we expect to go month after month without feeding our spirits on the Word of God? As healthy people, we would never starve ourselves to the point of malnutrition. Instead, we work hard to put healthy food on the table for our families—as well we should!

We need food to live and thrive physically. But many of us are spiritual anorexics. We starve ourselves of the Word of God. We think we can survive on a few crumbs of Scripture that we hear at church or on a Christian radio station. By going week after week without feeding on the Word, we are starving our spirits to the point of death.

Listen to what God said through Isaiah 55:2:

> "Why spend money on what is not bread, and your labor on what does not satisfy? Listen, listen to me, and eat what is good, and you will delight in the richest of fare."

We live in a world of spiritual famine today because we have malnourished ourselves into a spiritual coma. Do not become a spiritual anorexic. Decide today to feed every day on the Word of God.

2. Our Only Power for Living

It is said that, in one of the early New Year's Day Rose Parades in Pasadena, California, an elaborately decorated float sputtered to a stop in the middle of Colorado Boulevard. The truck that supported the float had run out of gas. The entire parade was stalled while the driver went to buy a can of gas. Even more embarrassing was that the float, sponsored by the Standard Oil Company, advertised Standard Oil's vast petroleum resources, yet someone had neglected to fill the gas tank.

This scenario could describe Christians who have access to God's vast resources through His Word but neglect to tap into that power. The Word of God is our only power for living. As Paul writes in Romans 1:16, "For I am not ashamed of the gospel, because it is the power of God that brings salvation to everyone who believes: first to the Jew, then to the Gentile."

We are always looking for power. When we feel weak and helpless, we want power over the circumstances and challenges of life. We sometimes look for power in self-help, how-to, or motivational books, and yet forget the one Book that is the source of power for living.

In God's Word, we find power over sin. We find power over temptation. We find power over our circumstances. We find power over this fallen world. When you need power, turn to God's Word.

3. Our Only Truthful Mirror

The Word of God is the only mirror that reveals the truth about us.

Reality is hard to face. Many of us—including many Christians—live in a fantasy world. We don't want to confront the reality of our transgressions, failures, habitual sins, or the times we have let friends and family down.

I was born in Egypt. The doctors told my mother there were complications in the pregnancy and advised her to undergo a therapeutic abortion. But our family pastor visited my mother and said God had told him that the child she carried would serve the Lord. So my mother rejected the doctors' advice and gave birth to me.

There were many times during my troubled boyhood when my mother must have wondered if our pastor had misheard the message from the Lord! I'm grateful to God that my mother lived to see me surrender my life to Him when I was sixteen.

But even after I committed myself to the Lord, I made it clear to my family that I did not want to go into the ministry. I thought I could still be a Christian while rejecting God's call on my life.

I wanted a successful career in the secular world, so I needed a university education. To enter university, I had to pass the high school certificate examination—a national exam that fewer than 38 percent of applicants passed. As the exam approached, I came down with typhoid. Suffering from a 105-degree fever, I took the exam without any hope of passing. I did pass—but with a score so low that no university would accept me.

I could either repeat a year of high school and try to bring up my score or join the military. I applied to the Egyptian Air Academy, hoping to become a flight navigator. Very few Christians are accepted, but the Academy approved my application. I convinced myself that God was in it and that He wanted me to serve Him in the secular workplace.

Two thousand cadets were accepted, and the Academy sent them letters, ordering them to report. But one of those letters got lost in the mail: mine. Weeks went by. Finally, I traveled to Cairo to find out when classes were to start. Upon my arrival, school officials told me that classes had started three weeks earlier—and I was held in contempt for showing up late.

By God's grace, a relative who was highly placed in the military intervened on my behalf. The Academy released me without punishment, but I still had to repeat my final year of high school.

Ironically, our family lived next to the university. Every morning, wearing my high school uniform, I had to walk past my former high school classmates as they were going in the opposite direction to their university classes. And every afternoon, I passed them again on my way home. It was the most embarrassing time of my life.

During those days of humiliation, God's Word spoke to me again and again. I thought of Jonah, fleeing from God's will only to face humiliation and despair in the belly of the fish. I thought of King David, forced into humiliating exile by his rebellious son Absalom, and later restored to the throne by God's grace. I thought of the Apostle Peter, a self-willed disciple who promised to remain faithful to death, then denied Jesus when accused by a lowly servant girl.

I identified with their humiliation. Reading their stories was like looking in a mirror. Throughout that humbling time in my life, I heard God saying to me, "Michael, I need you to obey My call on your life. Hear and obey—and I will honor you."

So I began to submit my will to God's will. Eighteen months later, I miraculously escaped from Egypt. Two years after that, I was enrolled at Moore College in Sydney, Australia, preparing for the ministry. God's Word rebuked me—but it also encouraged me to persevere in following His will for my life.

Today, I thank God that I lived long enough to look back and say, "Thank You, God, for my failures and humiliations." Why? Because

God was preparing me so that I could confront the truth about my life—and the truth of God's perfect plan for my future.

Mirrors Are Relentlessly Truthful

Looking into the mirror of God's Word can be an unpleasant experience. We don't like to be confronted with our hypocrisy. We don't want to admit to ourselves that we make moral compromises, that we are complacent and spiritually lazy.

Many of us feel guilty about our prayer lives. We tell ourselves, "I'll start praying daily. I'll build a habit of prayer." And we begin praying every morning and every night for a few days. And then we miss a day. Then two or three days. And soon we are back to our old prayerless lifestyle.

Or we feel guilty for neglecting the Bible. We tell ourselves, "I'll build a habit of meditating on God's Word." And we begin with the best of intentions. Then we miss a day, then two or three. And soon the Bible sits on the shelf, neglected.

We keep our commitment for a few days, but the change is temporary. God is looking for permanent change in our lives. Here's how I achieved that in mine.

In my early days as a pastor, I would run myself ragged trying to meet the demands of my ministry. I scheduled breakfast, lunch, and dinner meetings, and appointments all day long. But I neglected to schedule time with God in prayer and Bible meditation.

In 1993, I came down with double pneumonia. I was bedridden for two weeks—and during that time of illness, God convicted me that I should not minister to others until I had ministered to Him and to my own spiritual needs. From then on, I never made breakfast or early morning appointments. Instead, I always offered up the first fruit of my day to the Lord, praying and meditating in my Daily Chronological Bible.

If you struggle to make time for prayer and Scripture meditation, here are some suggestions:

1. *Pray through the Scriptures.* In the morning, pray these Scriptural prayers back to God: Psalm 5:2–3, Psalm 25:5, Psalm 90:14; Psalm 143:8, Lamentations 3:22–23, and 1 Thessalonians 5:17–19. In your intercessory prayers for others, pray through Ephesians 1:17–19, Ephesians 3:14–19, and Colossians 1:9–12. Write out those passages on a piece of paper or copy them into a file on your computer or phone to guide you through your prayers.

2. *Pray aloud.* There is something empowering and energizing about praying with your voice, not just your silent thoughts. You are truly conversing with the Father. Pray with the door closed and with no one listening but God. You'll pray freely, without feeling self-conscious. Your "prayer closet" may be your backyard, your basement, or a literal closet, but I encourage you to find a place where you can pray aloud to God.

3. *Begin with the Lord's Prayer.* I suggest adding three words— "in my life"—to three lines of that prayer: "Our Father in Heaven, hallowed be Your name *in my life.* Your Kingdom come *in my life.* Your will be done *in my life.*" You may find that these three simple words will personalize that prayer in a meaningful way. The Lord's Prayer also reminds us to ask God for our basic needs ("our daily bread"), for forgiveness and the grace to forgive others ("our debts" and "our debtors"), and for deliverance from temptation and evil. This is an effective pattern for prayer.

4. *Make a commitment.* Promise yourself and God that you will not start your day without your morning prayer and Bible meditation. Decide that your head won't hit the pillow until you

have met with God for your evening prayer and meditation. If you stick to that commitment for a few days, you will soon find that it becomes an unbreakable habit. You'll experience a new sense of victory in your walk with God.

God's Word holds up a mirror to show us what our spiritual life looks like. It can be painful to look in the mirror and face our physical imperfections. In the same way, it's painful to honestly look at ourselves in God's mirror, the Bible. We think, "If I don't look in the mirror, if I don't read the Bible, I won't have to acknowledge my flaws. I won't have to change."

Mirrors are relentlessly truthful. They take away our excuses. That's why James, the half-brother of Jesus, wrote:

> Anyone who listens to the Word but does not do what it says is like someone who looks at his face in a mirror and, after looking at himself, goes away and immediately forgets what he looks like. (James 1:23–24)

Do you enjoy looking in the mirror first thing in the morning? Is it pleasant to see your disheveled hair and your smooshed face? For me, facing the mirror is like a horror show. But that mirror gives me an honest reflection of myself. That reflection enables me to do something about that horror show before I go out and face the world. I can scrub my face and comb my hair and make myself presentable.

Now, suppose you look in the mirror and say, "Ugh! I don't like what I see. But I'm really busy today. I won't do anything about my appearance right now. Maybe tomorrow or next week." Then you go out your front door—and now you're a horror show for everyone who sees you. No rational person would look in the mirror and ignore what the mirror showed him.

But that's precisely what we do when we look into the mirror of God's Word, then ignore all the sins, flaws, and bad habits we find there. If we pretend we're doing just fine when God's Word says we're not, we gradually harden our hearts to the conviction of God's Spirit. The Bible is a mirror that reflects to us the reality of who we really are—not to condemn us, but to lead us to repentance and wholeness.

4. Our Only Cleansing Agent

Ephesians 5:25–26 tells us that "Christ loved the church and gave himself up for her to make her holy, cleansing her by the washing with water through the Word." No matter how dirty you feel, the moment you go under the shower of God's Word, you are 100 percent clean.

If the Bible were only a mirror to show us our wretched condition, where would we be? We would still be lost in sin. But thank God, His Word not only reflects reality but also cleanses completely. The Apostle Peter writes, "You have purified yourselves by obeying the truth" (1 Peter 1:22). By reading and studying the Word, we not only see the truth about ourselves but are also cleansed and purified. Obedience to God's Word is like a cleansing shower.

John R. W. Stott was rector of All Souls Church in London from 1950 to 1975. I first met him in 1971, and he became a friend and mentor to me until he went to be with the Lord in 2011. In his book *Issues Facing Christians Today*, he wrote:

> Our Christian habit is to bewail the world's deteriorating
> standards with an air of rather self-righteous dismay. We
> criticize its violence, dishonesty, immorality, disregard
> for human life, and materialistic greed. "The world is

going down the drain," we say with a shrug. But whose fault is it? Who is to blame?

Let me put it like this. If the house is dark when nightfall comes, there is no sense in blaming the house; that is what happens when the sun goes down. The question to ask is, "Where is the light?"

Similarly, if the meat goes bad and becomes inedible, there is no sense in blaming the meat; this is what happens when bacteria are left alone to breed. The question to ask is, "Where is the salt?"

Just so, if society deteriorates and its standards decline until it becomes like a dark night or a stinking fish, there is no sense in blaming society; that is what happens when fallen men and women are left to themselves, and human selfishness is unchecked.

The question to ask is, "Where is the Church? Why are the salt and light of Jesus Christ not permeating and changing our society?...The Lord Jesus told us to be the world's salt and light. If darkness and rottenness abound, it is largely our fault and we must accept the blame.[2]

Are we sick of the violence, immorality, and depravity of the world around us? Are we tired of being lied to by our political leaders? Have we grown weary of living behind prison bars of security doors and windows while lawless predators roam freely throughout the land? Are we disgusted with the filth and wickedness that passes for entertainment on our TV screens and streaming services? Are we alarmed by the godless indoctrination of our children in the public schools?

Do we want to see *revival* sweep across our land?

Then we need to confront the mirror that is God's Word. We need to feed on the nourishment of God's Word. We need to seek the daily power source that is God's Word. And we need to be washed and cleansed by God's Word.

Revival doesn't begin "out there," somewhere in society. Revival begins "in here," in your heart and mine, as we feed on the Word of God. I believe with all my heart that if you and I take God's Word seriously, we can truly reverse the corrosion and suicidal direction of our society. It all begins with you and me—and with the Word of God.

2

Two Testaments, One God

In his book *The God Delusion*, atheist Richard Dawkins illustrates a common misunderstanding of the Bible: the notion that there is a "God of the Old Testament" and a different "God of the New Testament." Dawkins writes, "The God of the Old Testament is arguably the most unpleasant character of all fiction" and a "capriciously malevolent bully."[1] (By the way, Dawkins might think calling the Bible "fiction" is a clever bit of mockery, but the inaccuracy of the statement only undermines his argument.)

Later in the book, Dawkins contrasts the God of the Old Testament with the God of the New Testament. He calls Jesus "one of the great ethical innovators of history," and adds, "The Sermon on the Mount is way ahead of its time. His 'turn the other cheek' anticipated Gandhi and Martin Luther King by two thousand years."[2] (To be accurate, Jesus didn't "anticipate" the nonviolent views of Gandhi and King. He *influenced* them.)

But are the New Testament teachings of Jesus at odds with the "God of the Old Testament"? Absolutely not. In the Sermon on the Mount, Jesus *intensifies* the demands of the Old Testament Law, and says,

> "Do not think that I have come to abolish the Law or the Prophets; I have not come to abolish them but to fulfill them. For truly I tell you, until heaven and earth disappear, not the smallest letter, not the least stroke of a pen, will by any means disappear from the Law until everything is accomplished." (Matthew 5:17–18)

And the love, grace, and mercy of God—which many people associate with God in the New Testament—are deeply rooted concepts in the Old Testament. According to the *Holman Bible Dictionary*, the Hebrew word for God's mercy, *chesed*, appears 245 times in the Old Testament, including 127 times in the Psalms. *Chesed* is also translated "steadfast love," "constant love," and "unfailing love" in various Bible versions.[3]

There are not two Gods in the Bible, an "unpleasant" God of the Old Testament and a merciful God of the New Testament. There is only one God. From Genesis to Revelation, His nature, character, and relationship with humanity is consistent and without contradictions. The Scriptures are unified from beginning to end, and they depict a single righteous and merciful God who is unchanging in all His ways.

Why then do so many people have a distorted perception of God? It comes from a superficial understanding of both the Old and New Testaments.

God's Old Testament Mercy and Compassion

If all we know of the Old Testament is a few isolated events, such as the Flood or the destruction of Sodom and Gomorrah, we will probably have an incomplete and wildly distorted perspective on God. People who criticize the "God of the Old Testament" as a "bully" ignore such Old Testament passages as these:

> Yet He was merciful;
> He forgave their iniquities
> and did not destroy them.
> Time after time He restrained His anger
> and did not stir up His full wrath.
> He remembered that they were but flesh,
> a passing breeze that does not return. (Psalm 78:38–39)

> Because of the LORD's great love we are not consumed,
> for His compassions never fail.
> They are new every morning;
> great is your faithfulness.
> I say to myself, "The LORD is my portion;
> therefore I will wait for Him."
> The LORD is good to those whose hope is in Him,
> to the one who seeks Him;
> it is good to wait quietly
> for the salvation of the LORD. (Lamentations 3:22–26)

God's wrath is righteous and just, but tempered with compassion. We see God patiently withholding judgment against sin throughout the Old Testament. The God of the Old and

New Testaments is consistently merciful. In fact, His justice
and anger are really facets of His compassion, because His
anger is directed at wickedness, injustice, oppression, and
murder. God judges wickedness out of His great compassion
for the innocent and the oppressed, as this Old Testament passage makes clear:

> There are six things the LORD hates,
>   seven that are detestable to him:
>   haughty eyes,
>   a lying tongue,
>   hands that shed innocent blood,
>   a heart that devises wicked schemes,
>   feet that are quick to rush into evil,
>   a false witness who pours out lies
>   and a person who stirs up conflict in the community.
>   (Proverbs 6:16–19)

The book of Psalms describes God as a protector of widows,
orphans, and the oppressed:

> You, LORD, hear the desire of the afflicted;
>   you encourage them, and you listen to their cry,
>   defending the fatherless and the oppressed,
>   so that mere earthly mortals
>   will never again strike terror. (Psalm 10:17–18)

Do these verses describe a "capriciously malevolent bully"—or
a God who protects the weak and oppressed? The compassionate
nature of our loving God drenches the Old Testament.

God's New Testament Wrath and Justice

Many people see "the God of the New Testament" as a God who winks at sin, does not judge wickedness, and makes no moral demands of humanity. In reality, the New Testament is filled with sober warnings about God's judgment of sin. There are several passages in the gospel accounts where Jesus thunders against sin and rebelliousness in terms that most people associate with the "God of the Old Testament." Here's one example:

> Then Jesus began to denounce the towns in which most of His miracles had been performed, because they did not repent. "Woe to you, Chorazin! Woe to you, Bethsaida! For if the miracles that were performed in you had been performed in Tyre and Sidon, they would have repented long ago in sackcloth and ashes. But I tell you, it will be more bearable for Tyre and Sidon on the day of judgment than for you. And you, Capernaum, will you be lifted to the heavens? No, you will go down to Hades. For if the miracles that were performed in you had been performed in Sodom, it would have remained to this day. But I tell you that it will be more bearable for Sodom on the day of judgment than for you." (Matthew 11:20–24)

In Acts 5, we meet two members of the early church, Ananias and his wife, Sapphira. The couple sold a piece of property and gave part of the money to the church. They said they gave all the money to the church, but they held some back. The Apostle Peter said,

> "Ananias, how is it that Satan has so filled your heart that you have lied to the Holy Spirit and have kept for yourself

some of the money you received for the land? Didn't it belong to you before it was sold? And after it was sold, wasn't the money at your disposal? What made you think of doing such a thing? You have not lied just to human beings but to God." (vv. 3–4)

And Ananias fell dead. Later, Sapphira also told the apostles that she and her husband had given all the money to the church. Peter said to her,

"How could you conspire to test the Spirit of the Lord? Listen! The feet of the men who buried your husband are at the door, and they will carry you out also." (v. 9)

And Sapphira fell dead also.

As a result of God's judgment against the lies of Ananias and Sapphira, "fear seized the whole church and all who heard about these events" (Acts 5:11). Make no mistake, the God of the Old Testament and the God of the New Testament are one and the same. He is a God who is patient, tender, compassionate, and loving—but He is also a God who judges sin.

The Bible, from Genesis to Revelation, is one harmonious story of God's love for sinners. His nature doesn't change over time. He is steadfast, faithful, and reliable. We can trust His perfect, unchanging character.

Both Testaments Agree on Salvation

Many Christians misunderstand the basis of salvation in the Old Testament. They think that people in Old Testament times were saved by keeping the Law of Moses and making sacrifices on altars. Nothing could be further from the truth. People in Old Testament times were saved on exactly the same basis as we are saved today: Salvation is a gift of God's grace which we receive through faith.

Genesis 15:6 tells us, "Abram believed the LORD, and He credited it to him as righteousness." In Romans, his great treatise on faith, the Apostle Paul writes,

> What does Scripture say? "Abraham believed God, and it was credited to him as righteousness."
>
> Yet he did not waver through unbelief regarding the promise of God, but was strengthened in his faith and gave glory to God, being fully persuaded that God had power to do what He had promised. This is why "it was credited to him as righteousness." (Romans 4:3, 20–22)

Abraham lived four hundred years before Moses. He didn't have the Law or the Ten Commandments. He could not have been saved by observing the Law and the sacrifices, which came centuries later. Abraham was saved by grace through faith.

If human beings could be saved by works, by keeping the Law and making animal sacrifices, then they would be able to boast of their own righteousness, their own works, their own observance of the Law. As the Apostle Paul states:

> For it is by grace you have been saved, through faith— and this is not from yourselves, it is the gift of God—not by works, so that no one can boast. (Ephesians 2:8–9)

Suppose someone in Old Testament times kept all the laws and made all the sacrifices, yet that person's heart was not right with God. Would those works save him? Of course not.

The same principle is true today. If a person goes to church every Sunday but has never surrendered in faith to Jesus Christ, will church attendance save him? Of course not. His heart is far from God. We can only be saved by grace through faith in Jesus Christ.

People in Old Testament times lived under the Old Covenant. Ever since Jesus introduced the New Covenant during the Last Supper, hours before the crucifixion, we have lived under the New Covenant. A covenant is a formal agreement. Under the Old Covenant, which God gave to the people through Moses, God's people demonstrated their faith by obedience to God's Law—and the symbols and sacrifices of the Law pointed forward to Jesus Christ. Under the New Covenant, our faith is in Jesus Christ and His sacrifice on the cross.

God made several covenants with His people in Old Testament times. In Genesis 12, He told Abraham (or Abram, as his name was then) to leave his country and go to a land that He would give him. He said,

> "I will make you into a great nation, and I will bless you;
> I will make your name great, and you will be a blessing.
> I will bless those who bless you, and whoever curses
> you I will curse; and all peoples on earth will be blessed
> through you." (see Genesis 12:1–3)

Later, God performed a covenant ceremony with Abraham involving animal sacrifice (see Genesis 15 and Hebrews 6:13–15).

God's covenant with Abraham was unconditional, a promise that required nothing of Abraham.

Later in Old Testament times, God made conditional covenants with Israel that required the people to meet certain standards. The clearest expression of a conditional covenant between God and Israel is found in Deuteronomy:

> So if you faithfully obey the commands I am giving you today—to love the LORD your God and to serve Him with all your heart and with all your soul—then I will send rain on your land in its season, both autumn and spring rains, so that you may gather in your grain, new wine, and olive oil. I will provide grass in the fields for your cattle, and you will eat and be satisfied.
>
> Be careful, or you will be enticed to turn away and worship other gods and bow down to them. Then the LORD's anger will burn against you, and He will shut up the heavens so that it will not rain and the ground will yield no produce, and you will soon perish from the good land the LORD is giving you. Fix these words of mine in your hearts and minds; tie them as symbols on your hands and bind them on your foreheads. Teach them to your children, talking about them when you sit at home and when you walk along the road, when you lie down and when you get up. Write them on the doorframes of your houses and on your gates, so that your days and the days of your children may be many in the land the LORD swore to give your ancestors, as many as the days that the heavens are above the earth. (Deuteronomy 11:13–21)

When some people hear terms like the "Law of Moses" or the "Old Covenant," they think only of the Ten Commandments. But God's covenant with Israel includes *all* the laws that He delivered to Israel in the first five books of the Bible, Genesis through Deuteronomy. When we speak of the Old Covenant, we speak of the covenant God made with Israel through Moses.

You might be surprised to learn that the concept of the New Covenant comes from the Old Testament. The prophet Jeremiah writes:

> "The days are coming," declares the LORD,
>   "when I will make a new covenant
> with the people of Israel
> and with the people of Judah.
> It will not be like the covenant
> I made with their ancestors
> when I took them by the hand
> to lead them out of Egypt,
> because they broke My covenant,
> though I was a husband to them,"
> declares the LORD.
> "This is the covenant I will make with the people of Israel
> after that time," declares the LORD.
> "I will put My law in their minds
> and write it on their hearts.
> I will be their God,
> and they will be My people.
> No longer will they teach their neighbor,
> or say to one another, 'Know the LORD,'

because they will all know Me,
from the least of them to the greatest,"
declares the LORD.
"For I will forgive their wickedness
and will remember their sins no more."
(Jeremiah 31:31–34)

The New Covenant was promised in the Old Testament. Jesus instituted it at the Last Supper when He took the cup and said, "This cup is the new covenant in My blood, which is poured out for you" (Luke 22:20; see also 1 Corinthians 11:25). With His death, Jesus became the mediator of the New Covenant, and His blood became the only blood sacrifice required under the New Covenant. In this way, Jesus fulfilled the promise God spoke through Jeremiah, "For I will forgive their wickedness and will remember their sins no more."

The Old Testament saints demonstrated their faith in God by keeping the laws and sacrifices that looked forward to the coming of the Messiah. As New Testament saints, we look backward to the sacrifice of Jesus on the cross—and we look forward to His return. Whether in Old Covenant times or New Covenant times, there has only been one way to be saved: by grace through faith alone.

Our unchanging God revealed Himself fully in Jesus Christ. That is why Jesus said, "Anyone who has seen Me has seen the Father" (John 14:9). No one before or after Jesus could make such a claim. As the Apostle Peter said,

Salvation is found in no one else, for there is no other name under heaven given to mankind by which we must be saved. (Acts 4:12)

Toss Out the Old Testament?

There is a common misconception in the church—and even among some Bible teachers and preachers—that the Bible contains two separate and largely unrelated stories. According to this mistaken view, the Old Testament is the story of Israel's history, the Law of Moses, and God's wrath and judgment—and the New Testament is the story of God's love, mercy, and grace through Jesus Christ.

Because of this misconception, many in the church have decided to toss out the Old Testament and preach only from the New Testament. They claim that the Old Testament is no longer relevant, and that all the teachings we really need for the Christian life are found in the New Testament. Yes, the New Covenant is superior to the Old Covenant because "the new covenant is established on better promises" (Hebrews 8:6). But the New Covenant does not invalidate the Old.

The death and resurrection of Jesus fulfilled the promises of the Old Testament—but Jesus did not change or erase any of the Old Testament promises. God did not change from one Testament to the next. The entire Bible is God's Word to us. It fully reveals God's love and His justice.

The Old and New Testaments complement each other. Neither Testament is complete without the other. Whether in the Old Testament or the New, every passage of Scripture points to God as our Creator and to Jesus as our Redeemer. The first Old Testament prophecy about Jesus is found at the beginning of the Bible, in Genesis 3:15, when God tells the serpent, "I will put enmity between you and the woman, and between your offspring and hers; he will crush your head, and you will strike his heel." The offspring of the woman is Jesus, who crushed Satan's head when He died upon the cross.

The renowned Bible scholar Alfred Edersheim identified 456 Old Testament verses that Jewish rabbis claimed were predictions about the coming Messiah or His times.[4] For example, Micah 5:2 predicted that the Messiah would be born in Bethlehem, and Zechariah 11:12 predicted that He would be betrayed for thirty pieces of silver. (For a partial list of messianic prophecies fulfilled by Jesus, see chapter 13.)

So the story of Jesus the Messiah does not begin in the gospel accounts in the New Testament. The first prophecy of Jesus appears in Genesis 3 and the prophecies of the coming Messiah are woven throughout the Old Testament.

Those who claim the Old Testament is no longer relevant are lopping off the first half of one continuous story of God's dealings with the human race. The New Testament must be understood within the context of everything that happened before.

The Old Testament tells why humanity needed a Messiah, where He would come from, what He would do, and why He would have to die for our sins. Those who would toss out the Old Testament are unwittingly attempting to shove Christianity off its foundation.

Understanding God's Judgment and Wrath

Many people reject the idea that God judges sin. But what if God allowed sin—including murder, violence, robbery, and oppression—to grow unchecked?

In the United States, we have seen what happens when sin and violence go unpunished. Sometime in the early 2000s, billionaire George Soros quietly began funneling money to political candidates running for district attorney in cities nationwide. Many voters had no idea what these well-financed candidates stood for, so they unwittingly voted for those who were soft on crime. Once in office, these district attorneys stopped prosecuting entire categories of crimes, including violent ones. They ended cash bail for arrested suspects, putting violent criminals back on the street the same day they were arrested.[5]

The predictable result was a 33 percent rise in the homicide rate in 2020 alone, with the trend line continuing to rise steeply ever since. Many businesses have been forced to close or leave areas where illegal activities have been decriminalized by radical prosecutors.[6]

It is righteous and compassionate to punish crime. God instituted government to protect the innocent. In a just society, evildoers should be afraid of the sword of government. As the Apostle Paul wrote:

> For the one in authority is God's servant for your good. But if you do wrong, be afraid, for rulers do not bear the sword for no reason. They are God's servants, agents of wrath to bring punishment on the wrongdoer. (Romans 13:4)

In the same way, God's judgment against sin is a function of His lovingkindness and mercy. The judgment and punishment of sin is a necessary part of a functioning society, whether in ancient Israel or in America today.

God's judgment is always just. Throughout the Bible, we see an all-wise God who maintains these two attributes—divine wrath and divine love—in perfect balance. In the Old Testament, God demonstrates a fatherly patience and compassion toward humanity (see Isaiah 54:10, Jeremiah 31:3, and Hosea 11:4). In the New

Testament, Jesus warns of the judgment to come—and He says that those who reject His gift of grace will be held accountable (see Matthew 11:21 and Revelation 20:11–15).

God's unchanging nature enables us to trust Him. In His Word, God testifies that He is unchangeable in all of His attributes:

> "I the Lord do not change. So you, the descendants of Jacob, are not destroyed. Ever since the time of your ancestors you have turned away from My decrees and have not kept them. Return to Me, and I will return to you," says the LORD Almighty. (Malachi 3:6–7)

God's plan for redemption also remains firm and unchanging. As God told Moses in Exodus 3:14, "I AM WHO I AM." And the New Testament tells us,

> Because God wanted to make the unchanging nature of His purpose very clear to the heirs of what was promised, He confirmed it with an oath. (Hebrews 6:17).

The Apostle James tells us,

> Every good and perfect gift is from above, coming down from the Father of the heavenly lights, who does not change like shifting shadows. He chose to give us birth through the word of truth, that we might be a kind of first fruits of all He created. (James 1:17–18)

A. W. Tozer aptly summed up God's unchanging character in his book *The Attributes of God*:

God never changes. What God was, God is. What God is and was, God will be. There will never be any change in God. Don't call me a heretic; check on me. Go to the Word and see if it's right....

There has been a lot of careless teaching that implies that the Old Testament is a book of severity and law, and the New Testament is a book of tenderness and grace. But do you know that while the Old Testament and the New Testament declare the mercy of God, the word *mercy* appears in the Old Testament over four times more often than in the New?...

The God of the Old Testament and the God of the New is one God. He did not change.[7]

What is the one major change between the Old Testament and the New? The unapproachable, holy God becomes approachable. In the Old Testament, God lives in unapproachable light. In the New Testament, God becomes a man, Jesus the Savior. Through the death of Jesus upon the cross, He brings peace with God to every man, woman, or child who calls on His name.

The Old Testament makes plain *our need* of salvation. The New Testament makes plain *God's plan* for salvation. In this way, the New Testament completes the Old Testament. We can depend on God to always be Himself. His plans never fail.

3

Rightly Dividing the Word of Truth

Menelik II was emperor of Ethiopia from 1889 until his death in 1913. He claimed to be a direct descendant of the biblical King Solomon and the Queen of Sheba (though there is no evidence in the Bible of a union between the two). Menelik II practiced the Ethiopian Orthodox Christian faith.

The emperor was apparently aware that Christians should feed on the Word of God. Matthew 4:4 tells us, "Man shall not live on bread alone, but on every word that comes from the mouth of God," and 1 Peter 2:2 says, "Like newborn babies, crave pure spiritual milk, so that by it you may grow up in your salvation." But the emperor didn't understand when the Bible should be taken literally and when it should be taken figuratively.

Whenever Menelik II had a headache or digestive disorder, his remedy was to tear a page or two from the Bible and eat it. He believed that literally "feeding" on the Word made him feel better.

In December 1913, the emperor suffered a stroke. He survived, and seemed to be recovering. But one day, he felt very ill. He ordered

his servants to bring out a Bible and feed him the entire books of
1 and 2 Kings, page by page. Before he could finish his meal of
Scripture, he collapsed and died.[1]

God has called us to feed on His Word as if our lives depend on
it. But God obviously intended that His Word should nourish our
minds and souls—not our digestive tracts. God gave us the Bible,
as Paul tells us in 2 Timothy 3:15, "to make [us] wise for salvation
through faith in Christ Jesus."

In that same letter, Paul told Timothy, "Do your best to
present yourself to God as one approved, a worker who does not
need to be ashamed and who correctly handles the word of truth"
(2 Timothy 2:15). In those days, before there was a recognized
canon of New Testament scriptures, the "Word of Truth" Paul
referred to was the Old Testament. Paul didn't dismiss the importance of the Old Testament—he *underscored* its importance.

In the King James Version, the phrase about a worker who "correctly handles the word of truth" is translated "rightly dividing the
word of truth." The original Greek word for "correctly handling"
or "rightly dividing" the Word of Truth is *orthotomounta*, a com-
pound word. *Ortho* means "right" or "straight," and *tomounta*
means "to cut." Literally, Paul is saying that the Bible must be
correctly cut (interpreted) in the same way that a skilled carpenter
would make straight cuts on a piece of wood.

Paul is not saying that we should "divide" the New Testament
from the Old and throw the Old away, as some tragically do. He is
saying we should interpret the entire Word of God rightly and with
precision—not in a careless or slipshod way.

I believe we now live in the days foretold by this Old Testament
prophecy:

"The days are coming," declares the Sovereign LORD, "when I will send a famine through the land—not a famine of food or a thirst for water, but a famine of hearing the words of the LORD." (Amos 8:11)

The Apostle Paul also foresaw a time when there would be a famine of the Word of God—not because there were not enough Bibles to go around, but because of neglect, apostasy, and a desire to have our biases confirmed. Paul wrote,

For the time will come when people will not put up with sound doctrine. Instead, to suit their own desires, they will gather around them a great number of teachers to say what their itching ears want to hear. They will turn their ears away from the truth and turn aside to myths. (2 Timothy 4:3–4)

May we never partake in a willful famine of the Word of God. The burden of my life is to equip you for the days that are coming upon us. The burden of my life is to teach God's people how to rightly divide the Word of Truth. Here are eight principles for correctly handling God's Word, both the Old and the New Testaments:

1. Ask the Holy Spirit to Open Your Understanding and Reveal His Truth

As you read, ask the Holy Spirit to guide your reading just as He guided the writing of the Bible. It is impossible to accurately understand God's Word without the illumination of God's Spirit. Filtering the Bible through our human intellect invites misunderstanding. As Paul told Timothy, "Reflect on what I am saying, for the Lord will give you insight into all this" (2 Timothy 2:7).

In my own human fallibility, I am prone to misunderstand and misinterpret God's Word. So whenever I open the Bible and study God's truth, I begin with an earnest prayer: "Holy Spirit, open my eyes that I may see wonderful truth from the Bible. Illuminate my mind so that I can discover the deep meaning You have for me in Your Word."

2. Avoid Proof Texting

What is proof texting? It means taking short passages of Scripture, sometimes a single verse, and giving it a "spin" or interpretation—usually different than the writer intended—to support a particular belief or doctrine. I often say, "Put the text in its context." When you quote a biblical text out of its context and offer it as proof that the Bible supports your position, that's proof texting. Instead of obeying God's Word, you are twisting Scripture to make it serve your purpose.

Here's an example: The Apostle Paul wrote,

> But [God] said to me, "My grace is sufficient for you, for My power is made perfect in weakness." Therefore I will boast all the more gladly about my weaknesses, so that Christ's power may rest on me. (2 Corinthians 12:9)

I have heard people quote this verse out of context and apply it to moral weaknesses. They say, "I used to struggle against the temptation to sexual sin or substance abuse or uncontrolled anger. But then I read that God's power is made perfect in weakness. So I don't need to struggle against temptation. I will just accept my moral weaknesses."

Now, it's obvious from the context that Paul is writing about physical weakness, about a chronic medical condition that would not heal. God told Paul to rely on His grace to endure the suffering he was experiencing. Paul was *not* encouraging people to give in to their moral weaknesses. But this is how some have twisted Paul's meaning through proof texting.

3. Know When to Take God's Word Literally or Figuratively

You might say, "I take the entire Bible literally!" But there are several places in Scripture where it would be a serious mistake to do so. There are certain linguistic principles that need to be observed, whether the passage was originally written in Hebrew, Aramaic, or Greek. If you don't understand these principles, you will misunderstand what God is saying to you.

In all Semitic languages (language groups that originated in West Asia and North Africa), there is something known as the "Hebraic hyperbole." It's the use of extreme, even absurd exaggeration to make a forceful point.

In Matthew 18:9, Jesus uses Hebraic hyperbole when He says, "And if your eye causes you to stumble, gouge it out and throw it away. It is better for you to enter life with one eye than to have two eyes and be thrown into the fire of hell." I know that a lot of Christians struggle with the temptation to sin with their eyes—but I have met very few one-eyed believers. So this is apparently a Bible passage most Christians interpret figuratively, not literally.

Jesus exaggerates to make a strong and important point. If your eye causes you to sin, please don't blind yourself. Instead, consider unsubscribing from that streaming service with all the immoral content that tempts you. Or ask a close Christian friend to hold you accountable for your internet viewing. Do whatever it takes to remove temptation from your eyes.

There are many ways to flee temptation and keep sinful images out of your mind without literally gouging out an eye. When you read Hebraic hyperbole in the Bible, don't take it literally—but by all means, take it seriously!

4. Understand the Historical and Cultural Context of Bible Passages

We are twenty-first-century people studying texts from distant times and places. We need to understand the cultural context of the passages we are studying.

The account of God sending Elijah to confront King Ahab and Queen Jezebel and the prophets of Baal still speaks to us today, even though it took place nine hundred years before Christ. We learn that all religions are not equal, and that the pagan gods (whether Baal or Ashteroth or Ashterah) are no match for the God of Israel. We learn that emotionalism and fervor (like the cries and chants of the pagan prophets) are not true signs of spirituality.

But we should not read about Elijah's challenge to the pagan prophets and then rush over to the local New Age center to challenge the guru to a contest of sacrifices. That's not what God wants us to learn from the life of Elijah. Instead, we should realize that our God is a mighty God, and He calls us to be witnesses for Christ in this godless culture, speaking His truth with the bold courage of Elijah.

Ask yourself, "What did this Bible passage say to the reader to whom it was written? When the ancient Hebrews or early Christians first heard this passage, how did they understand it? What was their cultural context? How did they apply this passage to their daily lives?"

But even though the Bible is one unified story, it has been told in numerous cultural contexts. Parts were delivered to the ancient Hebrews in the time of Moses, parts were delivered to the Jews living under the sway of the Babylonians or the Persians, and some parts were delivered to Greek-speaking audiences living under Roman oppression in Europe and Asia Minor.

For example, Moses was speaking to Israelites who had spent four hundred years surrounded by the idolatry of Egypt. They knew very little about Yahweh. They had no written Scripture, only oral traditions, so they had little knowledge of God. Moses had an enormous challenge trying to teach them about God as he led them out of Egypt. Even after God rescued them in the miraculous Red Sea crossing and provided them with manna in the wilderness, their understanding of Him was limited. That's important information to keep in mind when you see the Israelites repeatedly sliding back into idolatry and rebellion.

Centuries later, when Ezekiel and Jeremiah prophesied in Israel, they possessed written Scriptures. They had a lot of information about God. The prophets told the people again and again to remember the Lord who had rescued them from their enemies. The Israelites had received many blessings from God, yet they turned their backs on Him. They saw God perform miracles before their eyes, and yet they still wanted to worship Baal.

So it's important to understand that while Moses was talking to ignorant people, Ezekiel and Jeremiah were talking to rebellious people who rejected God's commandments. Understanding the intended audience for a certain passage of Scripture can help you to more accurately apply God's Word to your own life.

In the New Testament, we see that the Apostle Paul wrote letters, usually addressing specific problems, to various churches. The church in Philippi had very different problems from the church in Corinth or the church in Thessalonica. Paul dealt with each church and each issue in a specific and targeted way, and he gave each church biblical and godly answers. The better you understand the background of each church and the problems Paul was addressing, the better you'll understand what the Bible says about your own spiritual issues.

5. Use Study Aids to Improve Your Understanding of the Bible

There are many books on the market that can improve your understanding of God's Word—books for new Christians and beginning students of the Bible, books for young readers, books on Bible history, on theology, on individual books of the Bible, and on and on. I recommend that you read the Bible itself before turning to any of these study helps. Then turn to additional resources to deepen your appreciation of what you have read and meditated on.

Reading a passage in two or three translations can bring out shades of meaning you might miss by reading only one. To better understand the meaning of the original Hebrew and Greek words in the Bible, use online tools like Strong's Concordance with Hebrew and Greek Lexicons; you can search the Concordance at Eliyah. com/lexicon.html or StrongsConcordance.org. You can find many Bible translations and other study tools at BibleGateway.com.

6. Avoid Reading into the Bible What You Want It to Say

Ask yourself, "What does the Bible really mean here?" Try to clear away your preconceptions and biases. Try to read the Bible as if you are reading it for the very first time.

Approach God's Word with a willingness to be completely changed in your thinking and your way of life. The fallacy of reading into the text is called *eisegesis*, meaning the process of interpreting a text through the lens of your own biases and presuppositions. Instead of reading *into* the text, a good student of the Bible should read *out of* the text what is actually there. The process of setting aside our biases and reading out of the text is called *exegesis* (from a Greek word that means "to lead out").

Ask the Holy Spirit to illuminate your understanding. If you need more insight to understand the meaning of words or the cultural context of the passage, consult a trusted Bible commentary. Make sure you have a good grasp of what the Bible passage is saying to you.

7. Faithfully Apply What You Discover in the Bible

Ask yourself: "How can I apply this passage to my life today? How can I apply God's wisdom to my problems, my decisions, my challenges today? How can I apply these biblical principles to my business life, my home life, and my relationships?" Let the truth of God's Word penetrate every aspect of your life. Apply its truths to real-life situations.

Learning to faithfully apply God's truth to your life takes time. You cannot microwave the Scriptures, like heating up a cup of coffee. You simmer it slowly in the Crock-Pot of your thoughts and daily experience. When God speaks to you through a passage of

Scripture, write it on sticky notes and place it on your bathroom mirror, your refrigerator door, and the dashboard of your car. Live in that Scripture, memorize it, and let it bathe your mind—then look for opportunities to apply that Scripture in your everyday life.

Begin every day with the Bible open in front of you. As you explore the Bible, the Holy Spirit will point out areas of your life that should be brought under the authority of the Word. You'll begin to hear specific encouragement in the Word. You'll hear specific rebukes or challenges or warnings for your life.

Charles Spurgeon (1834–1892) was known as the "Prince of Preachers." Born in England, he was the longtime pastor of the New Park Street Chapel in London. He committed his life to Christ after a snowstorm forced him to take refuge in a church, where he heard the words of Isaiah 45:22: "Turn to me and be saved, all you ends of the earth; for I am God, and there is no other." Spurgeon did not have a long list of degrees after his name. In fact, he dropped out of school at age fifteen, taught himself to read Greek and Hebrew, and learned to read the Word of God in its original languages. He daily asked the Holy Spirit to open his mind and teach him truth from God's Word. Here is what Charles Spurgeon said about the Bible:

> Why, the Book has wrestled with me. The Book has smitten me. The Book has comforted me. The Book has smiled on me. The Book has frowned on me. The Book has clasped my hand. The Book has warmed my heart. The Book weeps with me and sings with me. It whispers to me and it preaches to me. It maps my way and holds up my goings. It was to me the Young Man's Best Companion and it is still my Morning and Evening

Chaplain. It is a living Book—all over alive—from its first chapter to its last word it is full of a strange, mystic vitality which makes it have pre-eminence over every other writing for every living child of God.[2]

This is a much-needed perspective on the Word of God. The Bible truly is a book with a "strange, mystic vitality." It is our sword that arms us for the spiritual battles we face every day, which are intensifying all the time. And the Word of God encourages us to keep fighting the good fight, because the Lord is on our side. We have read the last chapter, and it tells us that Jesus wins and He will establish His Kingdom forever.

8. Boldly Share God's Word

The best way to build the truth of God's Word into your life is to give it away at every opportunity. Share the good news of the Kingdom and the King. Tell others about some new morsel of truth you uncovered in your morning time of prayer and Bible study.

God will lead you to people who need to hear a message from His Word. Not everyone will accept it. Sometimes people won't want to hear about God's Word. Don't let rejection or opposition stop you. Now is the time to pray for boldness in sharing the good news with the people around us. We must pray for boldness rather than safety. We must obey God rather than human beings.

I believe we are only seeing the beginning of the opposition and persecution that is coming our way. We are heading for times of testing. Are we willing to stand for the truth and proclaim it in the face of persecution? Like the apostles of old, we need to share God's truth boldly and fearlessly, as if our lives depend on it.

The good news of the Kingdom won't win any popularity contests—but it is the truth. Let's proclaim it without compromise or hesitation, so that one day we can stand in the eternal Kingdom of our Lord Jesus and hear Him say, "Well done, good and faithful servant. Come and share your Master's happiness!"

PART II

The Kingdom and the Covenant

The themes of the Kingdom of God and God's New Covenant with humanity are woven throughout the Bible. If you know where to look, you can find these two themes in each of the sixty-six books of the Old and New Testament.

4

One King, One Kingdom

Rosalind Goforth (1864–1942) was an English-born Canadian author. She and her husband, Jonathan Goforth, served as missionaries to China. In a biography of her husband, *Goforth of China*, she tells the story of her conversion to Christ.

When she was twelve years old, she went to a revival meeting where an evangelist preached on John 3:16, in which Jesus tells Nicodemus, "For God so loved the world that He gave His one and only Son, that whoever believes in Him shall not perish but have eternal life."

Young Rosalind was deeply moved by the story of God's great love for all people. "I yielded myself absolutely to the Lord Jesus Christ," she wrote, "and stood up among others, publicly confessing Him as my Master."[1]

On the way home from the meeting, she told her parents that she had an absolute assurance that God loved her and had saved her. Her parents, however, told her it was foolish to think she could be certain that she was saved.

Troubled with doubts, she went home, opened her Bible, and started reading the Gospel of John. When she came to John 6:37, she found the assurance she was searching for in the words of Jesus: "Whoever comes to me I will never drive away."[2]

About a year after she publicly confessed Jesus as her Lord and Savior, young Rosalind and her sister were having breakfast on Easter Sunday. "It was so warm," she recalled, "only spring clothes could be worn. My sister and I decided at breakfast that we would not go to church, as we had only our old winter dresses."

She went to her room and took out her Bible, which she studied every morning. She opened it to Matthew 6 and read, "Why take ye thought for raiment [clothing]?...Seek ye first the kingdom of God, and all these things shall be added unto you" (Matthew 6:28, 33 KJV).

"It was as if God spoke the words directly to me," she wrote. "I determined to go to church, even if I had to humiliate myself by going in my old winter dress. The Lord was true to His promise; I can still feel the power the resurrection messages had upon my heart that day so long ago." As an extra gift of grace, the next day Rosalind received a package from her aunt. In the package were new spring dresses for herself and her sister.[3]

Rosalind Goforth experienced an unforgettable lesson in the importance of seeking the Kingdom of God.

Jesus told us that we should seek the Kingdom of God above all else—but what is the Kingdom of God? Many Christians have prayed the Lord's Prayer countless times without understanding what the phrase "Your Kingdom come" really means.

As we trace the concept of the Kingdom of God from the Old Testament through the New Testament, I believe your faith will be deepened and strengthened in a powerful new way. Let's grapple, as if our lives depend on it, with the biblical concept of the Kingdom of God.

A Tale of Two Kingdoms

Most people fix their hope on things that pass away. Many seek meaning for their lives by getting attention on social media. Others have invested everything in gaining success and wealth. As religious belief has declined in the Western world, many people have made politics their religion, as if the political kingdoms of this dying age are the only things that matter.

But a Christian who truly understands the priorities of God's Word has a very different focus. We do not fix our hope on things that are passing away—on worldly politics, wealth, or status. As Christians, we are called to seek first the Kingdom of God.

The Lord Jesus has promised us an eternal Kingdom in which He will one day transform everything. In His Kingdom, all the things people prize so highly will be less than a memory. Jesus's earthly ministry was focused on the Kingdom. The central theme of the Sermon on the Mount (Matthew 5–7) is that this world is wracked with poverty, injustice, sorrow, and persecution—yet through Jesus we possess the "Kingdom of Heaven" (a term He used interchangeably with the "Kingdom of God").

Jesus taught us to pray, "Our Father in heaven, hallowed be your name, your kingdom come, your will be done, on earth as it is in heaven" (Matthew 6:9–10). We are to pray continually that the Kingdom of God will come and that God's will would be done on earth.

Luke's gospel recounts a time when the Pharisees approached Jesus and asked when the Kingdom of God would come. Jesus replied,

> "The coming of the kingdom of God is not something that can be observed, nor will people say, 'Here it is,' or 'There it is,' because the kingdom of God is in your midst." (see Luke 17:20–21)

(The King James Version renders it "the kingdom of God is within you.")

In those amazing days when the crucified and risen Lord walked among the disciples, teaching them about the Kingdom, they still thought He was going to establish a political Kingdom of God on Earth. They were obsessed with the notion of a political messiah who would overthrow the Roman oppressors and restore Israel as it was in the days of King David and King Solomon.

So, in Acts 1, they asked Him, "Lord, are you at this time going to restore the kingdom to Israel?" Jesus replied,

> "It is not for you to know the times or dates the Father has set by His own authority. But you will receive power when the Holy Spirit comes on you; and you will be My witnesses in Jerusalem, and in all Judea and Samaria, and to the ends of the earth."

Moments after He said these words, He ascended into the clouds (see Acts 1:6–9).

The Pharisees, too, thought Jesus intended to establish a political kingdom. They repeatedly tried to trap Him into openly declaring Himself a political activist with ambitions to lead a rebellion against Caesar's rule.

When Jesus entered Jerusalem on Palm Sunday, riding on a donkey as foretold in Zechariah 9:9, the crowds praised Him and proclaimed Him their messianic King (see Matthew 21, Mark 11, and Luke 19). The religious leaders tried at first to silence the crowds. When that failed, they tried several times to trick Jesus into making a statement that would put Him in conflict with the Roman government.

In one of those encounters, the Pharisees and Herodians tried to trap Jesus into insulting Caesar by asking Him whether it was right to pay taxes. Jesus replied by pointing to Caesar's image on a coin, saying, "Give back to Caesar what is Caesar's, and to God what is God's" (Matthew 22:21). Jesus was saying, in effect, that Caesar ruled a secular political kingdom, but *His* was the Kingdom of God.

Jesus's Kingdom message came into sharp focus during His trial before Pilate, the night before the crucifixion. Pilate asked Jesus, "Are you the king of the Jews?" Jesus replied,

> "Is that your own idea, or did others talk to you about Me? . . . My kingdom is not of this world. If it were, My servants would fight to prevent My arrest by the Jewish leaders. But now My kingdom is from another place." (John 18:34–36)

Two Kingdoms

There are two kingdoms—the Kingdom of God and the kingdom of this world. You either belong to one or the other.

When we accept Jesus as our Lord and Savior, we are adopted into the Kingdom of God. We are eager for Him to rule over every aspect of our lives, right here and now. We are eager to see His Kingdom reign over the entire universe when Christ makes all things new. That is why Jesus taught us to pray, "Your kingdom come, Your will be done, on Earth as it is in Heaven."

As citizens of God's Kingdom, we are members of the royal family. We have intimate fellowship with the King of Kings because we are His children. Through prayer, we have access to God's throne. As Hebrews 4:16 tells us,

> Let us then approach God's throne of grace with confidence, so that we may receive mercy and find grace to help us in our time of need.

To become a citizen of another country, you must meet certain requirements. The Kingdom of God requires its citizens to accept the reign of King Jesus and to accept Him as Lord and Savior. It requires obedience to the Word of God. It requires us to say, "Not my will, but Yours be done."

Yet even as we pray that prayer, our selfish human nature creeps in. Instead of praying for God to live out His will in our lives, our prayers often revolve around our own egocentric ambitions and desires. Instead of seeking God's will, we try to bend His will to ours.

There is a war that rages within each Christian heart. It is a war between the Kingdom of God and the kingdom of this world. In Christ, we know we have the ultimate victory. But in this life, we know that our will, decisions, and even our prayers are a battlefield between the Kingdom of God and the kingdom of this world.

The better we understand the nature of God's Kingdom, as revealed in His Word, the better armed we will be to win this battle. Empowered by a knowledge of our role as soldiers of God's Kingdom, we press on—praying, obeying, and declaring His truth to a dying world.

Let's see what the Bible teaches about the Kingdom of God.

What Is the Kingdom of God?

The Kingdom of God is nothing less than the central theme of the Bible, the message that you and I are to proclaim to the world. The story of the Kingdom of God begins with Abraham. Hebrews tells us, "By faith Abraham...was looking forward to the city with foundations, whose architect and builder is God" (Hebrews 11:8, 10; see also Genesis 12). And the New Testament closes with the fulfillment of Abraham's hope in John's vision of "the Holy City, the new Jerusalem, coming down out of heaven from God" (Revelation 21:2).

We cannot fully grasp the gospel of salvation without understanding the Kingdom of God. In our study of individual books of the Bible, it's easy to miss the central theme that is woven throughout every book, from Genesis to Revelation. That central theme is the Kingdom of God.

Mark's gospel opens with the beginning of Jesus's ministry. There we find these significant words:

> Jesus went into Galilee, proclaiming the good news of God. "The time has come," He said. "The kingdom of God has come near. Repent and believe the good news!" (Mark 1:14–15)

The good news that Jesus preached was that the Kingdom of God had come. Wherever He preached, the Kingdom was on His lips. It was central to His teaching.

Many of the parables of Jesus were focused on the Kingdom of God. What is the Kingdom like? It is like a sower, Jesus said, who goes forth to sow seed. It is like a pearl of great price. It is like a mustard seed. How do you enter the Kingdom? You sell all that you have and give to the poor. You become like a little child.

Jesus spoke of the Kingdom of God again and again, yet He never paused to define it. Nor did any of His listeners interrupt Him to ask, "Master, what do you mean by the 'Kingdom of God'? Would you please define what this term means?" No, Jesus never defined this term. He assumed that all of His hearers knew what He meant—because they did. The Kingdom of God was a major part of the Jewish vocabulary. It was something they longed for deeply, even though their conception of the Kingdom was different from the Kingdom that Jesus proclaimed.

Today, many—if not most—Christians would be unable to define what the Kingdom of God is. They have heard the term before, but they would be hard-pressed to explain what it means.

The term "Kingdom of God" refers to God's rule over His people, and especially the fulfillment of His rule over all things at the conclusion of history. It will mean the end of all wars, all oppression, all enslavement, all racism, all crime, all sorrows, all tears. This is the Kingdom of God the Jews eagerly awaited.

The Jewish people were especially looking for a redeemer called the Messiah ("anointed one") who would establish the Kingdom of God in victory. When the New Testament declares that Jesus is the Messiah who has come to establish His Kingdom, we must look to the Old Testament in order to understand the messianic hope of Israel.

Let's trace the story of the Kingdom of God back to its origins in the Old Testament and the nation of Israel.

A Peculiar People

There were many tribes and nations on Earth when God established the nation of Israel, but its people were like no other people in the world. Israel's distinguishing feature was its unique religion, completely unlike the religions of all the surrounding Canaanite tribes. It was unique in two important ways:

First, the Jewish faith was *monotheistic*. The people of Israel served one God, and He had commanded them, "You shall have no other gods before me" (Exodus 20:3).

Second, the Jewish faith was *aniconic*, meaning the people were forbidden to make icons—representations of God in any human or animal form. Statues, carved images, and pictures were banned because God had commanded, "You shall not make for yourself an image in the form of anything in heaven above or on the earth beneath or in the waters below" (Exodus 20:4).

These two aspects of the Jewish faith contrasted sharply with the pagan religion of the surrounding Canaanite tribes. These ancient religions were *polytheistic*, meaning the people worshiped many gods, and *iconic*, because they used statues and images—icons—to represent them.

The pagan gods usually represented forces of nature (wind, water, fertility) or objects in the sky (the sun, the moon, the stars). The pagan gods were part of the natural order and did not demonstrate any moral character. They were not holy, all-knowing, or unchanging, like the God of the Jewish religion. In fact, many of the pagan gods were as unreliable and malicious as human beings. The pagans believed they could manipulate their gods into bestowing favors by means of rituals, chants, and sacrifices (including human sacrifices).

The God of Israel was completely unlike the pagan gods. The people of Israel knew Him as the one who created and controlled the sun, the moon, and the stars. The Jewish people also believed that God controlled human history, was righteous in His judgment, mighty in His saving power, and merciful in His fatherly love. There was no god in the pagan pantheon who was as powerful, good, and loving as the God of Israel.

God's name was written as four characters in the Hebrew language (known as the *Tetragrammaton*) which equate to YHWH in the English alphabet. Bible translators have transcribed YHWH as "Yahweh" or "Jehovah." In the Hebrew Bible, God has many other names as well, such as *El Shaddai* (Lord God Almighty), *Adonai* (Lord), *El* (God), *El Elyon* (God Most High), *El Olam* (Everlasting God), *Jehovah Nissi* (Lord My Banner), *Jehovah Rapha* (God Who Heals), *Jehovah Jireh* (God Will Provide), and *Tzevaot* or *Sabaoth* (Lord of Hosts), to name a few.

The people of Israel not only believed that God existed, but were convinced that He had entered history. They believed the Creator of the cosmos had spoken to Abraham and made a covenant with him: a promise to make a great nation, a chosen people, of Abraham's descendants. As you read through the Old Testament, it becomes clear that Israel was not chosen because of the people's intrinsic merit and sterling character; rather, the Exodus narrative is brutally honest in depicting a people who are ungrateful, unfaithful, and unworthy of God's grace.

God sovereignly and graciously chose a people for Himself so that they might choose Him.

Abraham and the Covenant in Blood

Our God is a covenant-making God. He made a series of covenants with the human race in both the Old and New Testaments. The covenants between God and human beings, however, are not like the agreements that you and I make with other human beings. A covenant between God and humanity is, by definition, a covenant between two unequal parties.

God made a covenant with Adam and Eve in Genesis 3:15. Immediately after the temptation and fall of Adam, God promised that Jesus the Messiah would come and crush the head of the serpent, the devil.

In Genesis 9:13–15, after God judged the world with a devastating flood, He made a covenant with Noah. He promised to never again destroy all life with a flood.

In Genesis 12:1–7, God made a covenant with Abraham. He called Abraham (or Abram, as he was then known) to leave Ur of the Chaldeans and move to Canaan. There, God promised, He would make a great nation of Abraham.

Then, in Genesis 15, God made another covenant with Abraham. Abraham had fallen into a spiritual depression and had begun to doubt God's promise. He wondered if God was going to keep the covenants He had made. God reassured him and said, "Do not be afraid, Abram. I am your shield, your very great reward"

(Genesis 15:1). God wanted Abraham to know that, regardless of any circumstances, He would keep His word.

When Abraham needed further reassurance, God showed him the countless stars shining in the night sky and said, "So shall your offspring be." Abraham didn't understand the full meaning of God's words. The Lord was speaking not only of Abraham's physical descendant, but of his spiritual descendants as well.

God credited Abraham's faith to him as righteousness. Over the centuries to come, God would also credit the faith of countless Old Testament and New Testament believers as righteousness. You and I as believers are the spiritual offspring of Abraham.

Next, God confirmed His identity to Abraham, saying, "I am the LORD, who brought you out of Ur of the Chaldeans to give you this land to take possession of it." Abraham loved God and honored God, but he still struggled with doubt. "Sovereign LORD," he said, "how can I know that I will gain possession of it?" (Genesis 15:7–8).

God knew that Abraham was weak in faith, just as you and I are weak in faith. In His mercy and kindness, God gave Abraham a visible sign of His covenant.

In the ancient Middle Eastern culture of Abraham, a covenant was sealed with a ceremony of sacrifice. People would kill an animal and cut it in half, then place the halves across from each other. The two parties of the covenant would walk on the bloody ground between the two halves of the animal. The symbolic point of this ritual was to say, "If I fail to keep this covenant, may what has been done to this animal be done to me. May I be cut in half."

In Genesis 15, God made a covenant with Abraham in precisely those Middle Eastern terms. It was a unilateral covenant in which

God took all the conditions on Himself and there were no conditions placed on Abraham.

As God instructed, Abraham arranged the halves of the slain animals. He drove away the birds of prey that tried to feed on the carcasses. Then, the Scriptures tell us, Abraham "fell into a deep sleep, and a thick and dreadful darkness came over him." Then God told Abraham that his descendants would be enslaved in a foreign land for four hundred years—but after that, they would "come out with great possessions." Abraham himself would be "buried at a good old age."

Then God entered the space between the animal halves alone, taking the visible form of a smoking firepot with a blazing torch. God made His covenant to Abraham through visible symbols, vowing to give his descendants a great land—far greater than modern Israel today, extending all the way to the Euphrates River in modern-day Syria and Iraq (see Genesis 15:9–20).

When God passed through the midst of the animals that were cut in half, He passed through the shed blood that soaked the ground—a foreshadowing of the blood of Jesus, which would one day be shed upon the cross. The blood of Jesus, which soaked the ground of Calvary, was the fulfillment of God's covenant with Abraham, saving us from sin and judgment.

The ceremony of the slain and divided animals was God's visible assurance to Abraham that He was not only a covenant-making God, but a covenant-keeping, God. As the New Testament tells us:

> When God made His promise to Abraham, since there
> was no one greater for Him to swear by, He swore by
> Himself, saying, "I will surely bless you and give you

many descendants." And so after waiting patiently,
Abraham received what was promised. (Hebrews 6:13–15)

We can trust the covenants and promises of God. When He
writes our names in His Book of Life when we receive Jesus as Lord
and Savior, He doesn't write with a pencil and erase our names
when we sin. He writes our names in the precious and indelible
blood of Jesus.

God often makes His promises visible to us in a memorable
way. When He covenanted with Noah after the flood, He gave the
sign of a rainbow. When Gideon asked God for a promise of victory
over the Midianites, God gave him the sign of a fleece spread out
on the floor. And when Jesus revealed the New Covenant that God
was making, He gave His disciples the visible, tangible elements of
Holy Communion, the bread (symbolizing His body) and the cup
of wine (symbolizing His blood).

The Law of the Old Covenant

Society today has lost sight of the solemnity of covenants and
keeping vows. Our culture treats morality and truth as matters
to be legislated or voted on. Nine black-robed justices can declare
the abortion of an unborn baby to be legally, morally acceptable. Legislators can pass a law or a majority of voters can pass
a proposition—and same-sex marriage can be declared legal and
moral. What's more, anyone who dares to oppose abortion or
same-sex marriage is accused of "hate."

But the universe is not interested in human opinions of what is
"moral" according to a majority vote. God has established moral
standards that are immutable and immovable. His standards are

not subject to an opinion poll or a judicial ruling. When it comes to God's moral law, only one opinion matters: God's.

The law of God is contained in what the Bible calls the "Law of Moses," which consists of the teachings of the first five books of the Bible—Genesis, Exodus, Leviticus, Numbers, and Deuteronomy. Judaism calls these five books the Torah (meaning "law"); in English, we call them the Pentateuch (meaning "five books" in Latinized Greek). The law was revealed to Moses by God. We see it called the "Law of Moses" for the first time in the book of Joshua:

> Then Joshua built on Mount Ebal an altar to the LORD, the God of Israel, as Moses the servant of the LORD had commanded the Israelites. He built it according to what is written in the Book of the Law of Moses—an altar of uncut stones, on which no iron tool had been used. On it they offered to the LORD burnt offerings and sacrificed fellowship offerings. There, in the presence of the Israelites, Joshua wrote on stones a copy of the Law of Moses. (Joshua 8:30–32)

After Moses led Israel out of Egypt, God gave His Law to Moses—a law that included moral instruction plus the specific rituals, requirements, and restrictions of the Israelite religion. Most of these instructions are found in the books of Leviticus and Deuteronomy. The priestly class, the Levites, were established as the keepers and interpreters of God's Law.

When God established His laws and commandments, He required perfect obedience. Does this seem like an unreasonable standard? No, it is not unreasonable—but it is unattainable. We can't hope to come close to God's standard of moral perfection.

That's why legalism—the attempt to save ourselves through the perfect observance of God's Law—is doomed to failure.

Fortunately for you and me, our God is not a legalistic God. He is a God of mercy and grace. That is why God sent His Son to die for our sins. Jesus came to meet all the requirements of God's Law. As Jesus Himself said, "Do not think that I have come to abolish the Law or the Prophets; I have not come to abolish them but to fulfill them" (Matthew 5:17). Jesus is the only human being who kept all of God's commandments all the time. He came to show us that the Law points to Him.

If Jesus came to fulfill the Law, why do we still need it? Shouldn't we ignore the Law of God and focus instead on the love of God? No. We still need God's Law because it is a mirror to see ourselves in. It shows us how far we are from God's perfect moral standard. It reveals our desperate need of a Savior. It shows us why Jesus had to die a lonely, agonizing, shameful death—the death of a criminal on the cross.

Jesus said, "For I tell you that unless your righteousness surpasses that of the Pharisees and the teachers of the law, you will certainly not enter the kingdom of heaven" (Matthew 5:20). At first glance, this is a terrifying statement because the Pharisees were meticulous about keeping the Law. The Pharisees even tithed from their spice racks, as Jesus said:

> "Woe to you, teachers of the law and Pharisees, you
> hypocrites! You give a tenth of your spices—mint, dill,
> and cumin. But you have neglected the more important
> matters of the law—justice, mercy, and faithfulness. You
> should have practiced the latter, without neglecting the
> former." (Matthew 23:23)

What did Jesus mean when He said that our righteousness must *exceed* that of the Pharisees or we cannot enter the Kingdom of Heaven? He wasn't advocating legalism. He was talking about the righteousness that flows from the grace of God as a free gift. The righteousness that is greater than that of the Pharisees is the perfect righteousness of Jesus that we receive when we commit our lives to Him.

The Letter and Spirit of the Law

We cannot earn our way into heaven by good works. We must accept the free gift of salvation by grace through faith. Does this mean that, once we are saved by grace, we can break the commandments without worry or guilt? Absolutely not! Anyone who believes that way and lives that way is certainly not saved by grace.

We have been saved so that Jesus Christ might live His life through us. If Christ lives in us, and if we obey Him out of gratitude for the salvation He gives us, we will not be habitual lawbreakers. As the Apostle John wrote:

> We know that we have come to know Him [Jesus] if we keep His commands. Whoever says, "I know Him," but does not do what He commands is a liar, and the truth is not in that person. But if anyone obeys His word, love for God is truly made complete in them. This is how we know we are in Him: Whoever claims to live in Him must live as Jesus did. (1 John 2:3–6)

If we truly belong to Christ, we want to obey God. Grace gives us the desire and the power to obey God. Yes, we will fail and we will sin—but we will know in our consciences that we are wrong. We will repent and confess our sins and receive His forgiveness.

Once we have experienced the grace of God, we will want to obey Him. We may not always keep the letter of the Law, but we will always want to keep the spirit of the Law. Not only will we refuse to commit adultery, but we will feel convicted if we even look at someone with lustful thoughts. We will not merely reject revenge—we will actively forgive those who have hurt us. We will love our enemies because love is the spirit of the Law.

Jesus did not abolish the Law of God. He fulfilled it so that our righteousness could be greater than the righteousness of the Pharisees. Our righteousness is the righteousness of Jesus Himself.

5

The Six Biblical Covenants Jesus Fulfilled

Throughout the Old Testament, God made a series of covenants. Each covenant revealed more details of God's perfect plan to establish His eternal Kingdom and redeem His people. Jesus the Messiah, whom the prophet Isaiah called Immanuel ("God with us") (see Isaiah 7:14), has fulfilled all of God's covenants with the human race. Let's explore each one in turn.

1. God's Covenant with Adam

In Genesis 3:15, after Adam sinned and fell from a state of obedient innocence to a state of sinful depravity, God promised that a Son of Adam's race would achieve victory over Satan. In the presence of Adam and Eve, He told the serpent—who was Satan—"I will put enmity between you and the woman, and between your offspring and hers; he will crush your head, and you will strike his heel."

In the Garden of Eden, God provided Adam and Eve with a beautiful garden, satisfying work, delicious food, and companionship with each other—and companionship with Himself. Adam and Eve yielded to temptation, rejected God's plan for their lives, and fell under the curse of sin and death. Despite their unfaithfulness, God promised them the ultimate victory through the coming Savior—a covenant that Jesus fulfilled on the cross.

2. God's Covenant with Noah

To fulfill His promise to Adam, God had to sustain and protect mankind from moral corruption and extinction. When wickedness and violence became rampant in the human race, God decided to use a flood to cleanse the earth of human evil. Yet He also chose Noah to be a new Adam on this new earth—a man who, along with his family, would preserve the human race from extinction. After the flood, God blessed Noah and his sons, saying, "Be fruitful and increase in number and fill the earth" (Genesis 9:1). In this way, God made sure that the offspring of Eve—Jesus the Messiah—would one day be born to fulfill the covenant He had made with Adam.

3. God's Covenant with Abraham

In Genesis 12:1–3, God called Abraham (who was then known as Abram) out of the city of Ur in the land of the Chaldeans and promised to make him the father of a great nation. "I will make your name great," God said, "and you will be a blessing. I will bless those who bless you, and whoever curses you I will curse; and all peoples on earth will be blessed through you."

Later, in Genesis 15, when Abraham was old and his wife was childless, God reconfirmed His promise, saying, "Look up at the sky and count the stars—if indeed you can count them. So shall your offspring be." And the Scriptures tell us that Abraham believed God, and God accounted his faith as righteousness.

In Genesis 17, when Abraham was ninety-nine years old, God appeared to him and reaffirmed His covenant, saying,

> "You will be the father of many nations. No longer will you be called Abram; your name will be Abraham, for I have made you a father of many nations. I will make you very fruitful; I will make nations of you, and kings will come from you. I will establish My covenant as an everlasting covenant between Me and you and your descendants after you for the generations to come, to be your God and the God of your descendants after you. The whole land of Canaan, where you now reside as a foreigner, I will give as an everlasting possession to you and your descendants after you; and I will be their God." (vv. 4–8)

Over and over again, God demonstrated that His covenant would not fail, even when Abraham was nearing a century in age. Why? Because it wasn't up to Abraham to keep the covenant. It was up to God, who promised in sacrificial blood—blood that pointed to the ultimate sacrifice of Jesus—that He would keep His promise.

4. God's Covenant with Moses

In Exodus 19–31, God promised never to forsake His people—and He foreshadowed the once-and-for-all sacrifice of the coming Messiah. By that time, Abraham's descendants had become slaves in the land of Egypt. But God displayed His sovereign power with a series of miracles that culminated in Moses leading the people out of Egypt.

In the wilderness, God gave them the Law, the Tabernacle, and the ritual sacrifices, all of which made clear the impossibility of redemption without God. His covenant with Moses has often been misinterpreted as a works-based righteousness. But in reality, the rituals and sacrifices demonstrated to the people that the terrible cost of sin included death and the shedding of blood. The blood of animals could never atone for sin once and for all. Instead, the animal sacrifices pointed to the grace of God and the promised Savior who was to come.

5. God's Covenant with David

In 2 Samuel 7, God speaks through the prophet Nathan and gives King David a promise that the everlasting King, the coming Savior, will one day be born from the lineage of David. God had established David as a king after His own heart: "The LORD has sought out a man after His own heart and appointed him ruler of His people" (1 Samuel 13:14).

Later, when David brought the Ark of the Covenant back to Jerusalem, God gave him an amazing promise—He promised to establish his throne forever. And though God would discipline David's descendants when they strayed, His gracious love would never depart from his house.

One day, the perfect, sinless King would come, born of a virgin of the lineage of David. He would be pierced and forsaken in our place. The punishment we deserve would be meted out upon Him.

6. The New Covenant

The New Covenant is God's promise to redeem forever all who call upon the name of Jesus for salvation. Under the New Covenant, it is not just the people of Israel who are chosen by God. Instead, all who believe are now God's chosen people. The New Testament book of Hebrews quotes from the Old Testament book of Jeremiah:

> "The days are coming, declares the Lord,
>   when I will make a new covenant
> with the people of Israel
>   and with the people of Judah....
> I will put My laws in their minds
>   and write them on their hearts.
> I will be their God,
>   and they will be My people.
> No longer will they teach their neighbor,
>   or say to one another, 'Know the Lord,'
> because they will all know Me,
>   from the least of them to the greatest.
> For I will forgive their wickedness
>   and will remember their sins no more."
> (Hebrews 8:8, 10–12)

The New Covenant is not an idea that was invented in New Testament times. It was part of God's plan from the very beginning.

God announced it through the Old Testament prophet Jeremiah. It was always His plan to send His Son, Jesus the Savior, to become the perfect sacrifice for the forgiveness of sin.

Jesus fulfilled each covenant. He humbled Himself to be born a man, according to God's promise to Adam. He came from the line of Abraham. He fulfilled the Law of Moses, pouring out His blood as the perfect sacrifice for our sin. He came as a King of the line of David. He instituted the New Covenant in His blood. On the cross, He defeated sin and death, once and for all—and He will come again to bring His people into the new Promised Land where God will dwell with them forever.

6

David and Solomon: Foreshadowing God's Kingdom

John Ashcroft has served as governor of Missouri, a United States senator, and U.S. attorney general. The morning Ashcroft was to be sworn in as senator in January 1995, he joined friends and family at a house near the Capitol building for a dedication service.

One of those present was Ashcroft's father, James Robert Ashcroft, a retired minister who was in poor health due to a heart condition. He had confided to a friend that he was dying, but wanted to see his son sworn in.

The attendees sang a few hymns, then Ashcroft's father said, "John, please listen carefully. The spirit of Washington is arrogance, and the spirit of Christ is humility. Put on the spirit of Christ. Nothing of lasting value has ever been accomplished in arrogance."

The attendees knelt in front of the sofa where John's father sat. As they placed hands on John to anoint him with oil and prayer in the way of the ancient kings of Israel when they undertook their administrative duties, the senior Ashcroft struggled to rise.

Concerned, John said, "Dad, you don't have to stand."

"John," his father said, "I'm not struggling to stand. I'm struggling to kneel."

John never forgot those words, which were among his father's last; he died later that night.

Ashcroft's father taught him that a genuine leader doesn't struggle to stand—that's the posture of arrogance. A genuine leader struggles to kneel in prayer and humility.[1]

Israel's kings still speak to us from the pages of God's Word. King Saul, it may be said, was a leader who struggled to stand, a king who led in arrogance. But King David was a leader who struggled to kneel. The Kingdom of Israel that God established through David was a foreshadow of that future eternal Kingdom whose Ruler would inherit David's throne, Jesus the Lord.

A Man after God's Own Heart

Speaking through the prophet Samuel, God declared, "I have found David son of Jesse, a man after My own heart; he will do everything I want him to do" (see Acts 13:22 and 1 Samuel 13:14). David was an imperfect man and an imperfect leader, yet God declared him to be a man after His own heart. There are several reasons why God made this declaration.

First, David was humble. Though he was the king, he had no exaggerated sense of his own importance. When the prophet Nathan told him:

> "The LORD declares to you that the LORD himself will
> establish a house for you: When your days are over
> and you rest with your ancestors, I will raise up your

offspring to succeed you, your own flesh and blood, and
I will establish his kingdom. He is the one who will build
a house for My Name, and I will establish the throne of
his kingdom forever." (2 Samuel 7:11–14)

David humbly prayed, "Who am I, Sovereign LORD, and what
is my family, that you have brought me this far?" (v. 18).

Second, David loved God's Word. Every verse of Psalm 119 is
shout of praise for it. Here is a typical passage:

Oh, how I love your law!
 I meditate on it all day long.
Your commands are always with me
 and make me wiser than my enemies.
I have more insight than all my teachers,
 for I meditate on your statutes. (Psalm 119:97–99)

David was a man after God's own heart because he fed his soul
on the thoughts of God.

Third, David loved and trusted God. Because of the Psalms he
composed, we have more insight into his soul than that of almost
any other person in Scripture. David was deeply aware of his own
sins, and he was grateful to God for the blessings of forgiveness.
He wrote:

Blessed is the one
whose transgressions are forgiven,
whose sins are covered.
Blessed is the one
whose sin the LORD does not count against them

and in whose spirit is no deceit....

Rejoice in the LORD and be glad, you righteous;

sing, all you who are upright in heart! (Psalm 32:1–2, 11)

David knew that God saw him as righteous—not because he never sinned, but because he loved God and repented from his sins.

Fourth, David demonstrated Christlike love. His predecessor, King Saul, was an insecure, jealous, and violent man who attempted to kill David several times (see 1 Samuel 19–24). David responded to Saul's attempts on his life with forgiving, Christlike love. A thousand years before Jesus preached the Sermon on the Mount, David lived out the Lord's command, "Love your enemies and pray for those who persecute you" (Matthew 5:44).

One reason we know we can trust God's Word is that it tells us the unflattering truth about its heroes. David was one of the greatest leaders in history, yet the Bible honestly reveals his moral failures. Can you imagine what it would be like to be David, to have not only your triumphs recorded, but also your acts of disobedience, adultery, and murder enshrined in God's eternal Word for millions to read, generation after generation, century after century?

God's Word is trustworthy and true. That's why it still speaks to us today.

The Origin of Israel's Monarchy

The Israelite people originated as an ethnic and religious community in the Middle East during the second millennium before Christ. Their ancestry begins with the patriarch Abraham, his son Isaac, and Isaac's son Jacob. God gave Jacob the name "Israel" after he successfully wrestled with the angel of the Lord (see Genesis

32:28 and 35:10; see also Hosea 12:5). The Twelve Tribes of Israel are descended from the twelve sons of Jacob.

Jacob's son Joseph was sold into slavery in Egypt, and he later rose to become Pharaoh's right-hand man. At the behest of Pharaoh himself, Jacob and his family moved to Egypt to live with Joseph. The descendants of Jacob were later enslaved in Egypt for four hundred years. The enslavement of Jacob's descendants, the Israelites, ended when Moses led them out of Egypt. In the wilderness, God gave His Law to Moses.

After Moses died, his successor, Joshua, led the Israelites out of the wilderness. They crossed the Jordan River and conquered the Promised Land—the land God had given them according to His covenant with Abraham. At that time, Israel was not a true nation. It had no borders or central government. Israel was a loose confederation of clans ruled by local elders. These clans were united by their common worship of one God.

During this time, the Israelites occasionally flirted with the idea of having a king. In the book of Judges, after Gideon led Israel to victory over the Midianites, the people said to Gideon, "Rule over us—you, your son and your grandson—because you have saved us from the hand of Midian."

But Gideon refused to be the king of the Israelites. "I will not rule over you," he said, "nor will my son rule over you. The LORD will rule over you" (see Judges 8:10–23).

Over time, the people increasingly clamored for a king. It wasn't enough for them to be ruled by God. Now they definitely wanted a monarchy. Why? Because that's the way pagans were ruled. Israel's demand for a monarchy was a flagrant rejection of Yahweh's authority—and that is one reason why the prophets rose up and condemned the idea of monarchy for Israel.

Meanwhile, the Philistines—a fierce, well-armed people—began to menace the Israelites. In their first few clashes, the people of Yahweh were crushed. This emergency led the Israelites to demand the leadership of a king.

The book of 1 Samuel records that a man named Saul, a member of the tribe of Benjamin, was anointed king by the prophet Samuel. In spite of Saul's bold courage, he lacked the mental and emotional stability to unify and lead his people. Although his reign would end in failure, Saul's kingship eased Israel through the transition from a tribal society to a true nation-state.

The Ascendance of David

During a battle with the Philistines at Mount Gilboa, King Saul saw that the battle was lost. First, the Philistines killed three of his sons, then grievously wounded Saul himself. When Saul's armor bearer refused an order to kill him as an act of mercy, Saul fell on his own sword and died by suicide.

Afterward, David (who had married Saul's daughter Michal) contended with Saul's son Ish-Bosheth for the throne. David prevailed and ascended to the throne of the unified kingdom of Israel and Judah.

Under David's able leadership, the nation of Israel was saved, the people experienced peace and prosperity, and the kingdom rose to unprecedented heights of glory. His reign fully justified the chants of praise: "Saul has slain his thousands and David his tens of thousands" (1 Samuel 18:7).

King David's policies transformed Israel from a beleaguered fiefdom into a dominant military power. As a warrior-king, David led his people from one victory to the next. He unified the bickering tribes and conquered Jerusalem, which contained the fortress of Zion. He made Jerusalem the capital of a mighty Israelite empire that stretched from the Gulf of Aqaba in the south to central Syria in the north. Kings came from all over the world, eager to make peace treaties with the mighty King David.

In 2 Samuel 8, we see such statements as "The Moabites became subject to David and brought him tribute," "the Arameans became subject to him and brought tribute," and stories of silver, gold, and bronze that David plundered from "Edom and Moab, the Ammonites and the Philistines, and Amalek" and on and on. David clearly believed that Israel's enemies should finance its economy, and that the Israelite people should be prosperous and lightly taxed. In the Psalms, David wrote of his people,

> You will eat the fruit of your labor; blessings and prosperity will be yours. (Psalm 128:2)

Though David began his reign as a warrior-king, never hesitating to fend off foreign threats so that his people might live in peace, he didn't see war as the way to achieve national prosperity. In Psalm 144, he revealed that he was eager to build a strong peacetime economy by faithfully obeying God:

> From the deadly sword deliver me;
> rescue me from the hands of foreigners
> whose mouths are full of lies,
> whose right hands are deceitful.
> Then our sons in their youth

will be like well-nurtured plants,
and our daughters will be like pillars
carved to adorn a palace.
Our barns will be filled
with every kind of provision.
Our sheep will increase by thousands,
by tens of thousands in our fields;
our oxen will draw heavy loads.
There will be no breaching of walls,
no going into captivity,
no cry of distress in our streets.
Blessed is the people of whom this is true;
blessed is the people whose God is the LORD.
(Psalm 144:11–15)

Under the leadership of King David, and later his son, King Solomon, Israel achieved unrivaled heights of power and prestige. The Bible tells us that ships brought cargoes of gold, precious stones, and construction-grade timber from Ophir, much of which was used to build the great Temple in Jerusalem. Israel traded with merchants and Arabian kings, and King Solomon hosted a state visit from the Queen of Sheba. The wealth of the Davidic State was unlike anything the world had ever seen (see 1 Kings 10:11–29).

The people were proud to be subjects of the kingdom. To them, the power and splendor of Israel must have seemed like the fulfill-ment of God's promise to Abraham: "I will make of you a great nation" (Genesis 12:2). They probably thought they were living in the Kingdom of God. However, though God had blessed and defended the nation, Israel was not the biblical Kingdom of God. It was an earthly kingdom ruled by fallible human leaders.

The Fall and Redemption of David

The Bible lays out the story of David and Bathsheba with shocking candor in 2 Samuel 11 and 12. Even more surprising, David *himself* confesses his sin before the entire nation in the inscription of his psalm of repentance: "A psalm of David. When the prophet Nathan came to him after David had committed adultery with Bathsheba" (Psalm 51:1).

The Bible tells us that, in the springtime, "when kings go off to war," David wasn't where he belonged, on the battlefield with his army. Instead, he was on his palace roof, where he saw a woman bathing. Instead of looking away, he stared at her, lusted for her, and sent for her. She was Bathsheba, married to Uriah the Hittite, a high-ranking soldier who was on the battlefield, doing his duty for his king. David committed adultery with Bathsheba and she became pregnant. To cover up his sin, he arranged for Uriah to be killed in battle—a case of cold-blooded murder.

Bathsheba mourned for Uriah, and David brought her into the palace and made her his wife. "But the thing David had done displeased the LORD" (2 Samuel 11:27). But He loved him too much to not allow David to remain in his unrepentant state. God sent Nathan the prophet to confront David's hidden sin and hypocrisy (see 2 Samuel 12). After hearing Nathan's accusation, David fell on his face and repented.

God forgave David's sin—but the consequences of it went on and on. The child born of the adulterous union died seven days after he was born. Afterwards, David's kingdom was beset by enemy nations. One of his own sons, Absalom, later rebelled and brought him calamity, as Nathan predicted. The grievous consequences of David's sin remained with him the rest of his life.

Even so, after David confessed his sin and repented, God forgave him and gave him a second chance in the form of an heir, Solomon, David's second son with Bathsheba. Solomon is proof that God forgave and restored David by His great mercy and grace. The past and its consequences could not be undone, but God could still rewrite David's future by giving him a son to carry on his work of establishing the Temple and expanding the kingdom of Israel.

There's an instructive scene in David's life. It takes place before he became king, when he was a fugitive from Saul's wrath and began recruiting an army. The warriors came from many tribes—brave men, ready for battle. But the Bible describes the tribe of Issachar with this fascinating statement: they were "men who understood the times and knew what Israel should do" (1 Chronicles 12:32).

This historical detail demands our attention. The men of Issachar understood the times in which they lived and they knew the direction their nation should go. This is a special form of wisdom and insight that we desperately need today. We need to discern the condition of our society in these dark and troubling times—and we need to understand how God is calling us as Christians to respond.

In order to do this, we need a deep knowledge of the mind of God. He has expressed His will for the world through His Word. The tragedy of the Church in the twenty-first century is that our knowledge of the Bible is abysmal. We have neglected God's Word for so long that we don't even realize how far we have fallen—and how urgently we need to repent.

Interrogating God's Word

Today, thanks to the internet, the world is flooded with information as never before—and most of that information is useless, misleading, or downright destructive. But in the meantime, biblical illiteracy is epidemic throughout the world, and even within the Church.

In past eras, even nonbelievers considered it important to have some biblical knowledge. You could not be considered a cultured and educated person without some knowledge of the Bible. In today's postmodern culture, however, the Bible is reviled. Even in many churches, those who love and obey God's Word are labeled with "woke" terms of contempt such as "heteronormative," "patriarchal," "sexist," "white supremacist," and "oppressor."

In one major New York City church, in October 2022, a preacher interpreted the story of David and Bathsheba through the lens of "woke" progressive ideology, saying, "David lay with Bathsheba and had her husband murdered after impregnating her. So does one horrible, despicable act wipe out all the good David has done?" He gave an exaggerated shrug. "At the very least, it complicates things. But for me, I don't trust this character. I don't trust his story or his repentance.... Now I know the tradition teaches us that David recognizes his sin and repents. Good for him." Those last three words drip with sarcasm.

"But what about Bathsheba?" he continued. "Because I also know that the tradition favors men. The tradition favors whiteness. The tradition favors wealth and protects those with power. And quite frankly, the tradition has given us a world that continues to prop up attitudes and behaviors that are death-dealing to women and girls, to indigenous siblings, to LGBTQ-plus people in our community, to folks of color and culture."

What "tradition" was the preacher referring to? The "tradition" of teaching stories from God's Word.

"Ancient stories like this one," the preacher continued, "unexamined and uninterrogated, give cover to men who send messengers to get women. And why does David get to be the only one called a man after God's own heart? What does that say to women and girls? And what does that say to other men and boys? And the question I really don't want to ask: What does that say about God?"[2]

This kind of "preaching" is becoming increasingly common in churches today— "preaching" that doesn't proclaim God's Word, but interrogates it; that doesn't draw spiritual lessons from the failings of Bible heroes, but seeks to cancel and demonize them; and that doesn't merely ask questions about God, but calls God into question.

Postmodern deconstructionism has invaded every aspect of our culture like a metastatic cancer. It has even spread its poison into the church. It is replacing the biblical worldview with a satanic program of deconstructing and erasing God's Word.

Christians who love the Bible have a clear understanding of David's life, both his high points and his tragic failings. I have never heard any Bible-believing Christian say, "David was guilty of lust, adultery, and murder—and his story gives me permission to let my own sinful passions run riot!" A true understanding of God's Word enables us to be repelled by the awfulness of sin while making room for redemption and forgiveness. This balanced view of human nature is something the worldly, postmodern, "woke" mind cannot understand.

God calls us to be like the warriors of the tribe of Issachar, people who understand the times and know what to do. We need to be people of God's Word, because only there do we find a true understanding of the times in which we live, and only in its principles can we learn how God is calling us to respond.

The Rise and Fall of King Solomon

David's son, King Solomon, was famed for his wise leadership and writing three books of the Bible—Proverbs, Ecclesiastes, and Song of Solomon. But he also had seven hundred wives and three hundred concubines, including Pharaoh's daughter and foreign princesses from Moab, Ammon, Edom, and other nations. Solomon allowed his foreign wives to bring their gods to Israel—and he even built temples to these foreign deities. According to 1 Kings 11:4, as Solomon grew old, his pagan wives "turned his heart after other gods, and his heart was not fully devoted to the LORD his God, as the heart of David his father had been."

Solomon had inherited a nation built on the spoils of war and the riches of tribute paid by other nations. He faced the challenge of growing Israel's economy through trade—and growing the government through taxation (see 1 Kings 4:7, 10:14–15; 1 Kings 12:3–4). He also launched a building program that he hoped would increase national unity and pride. To provide labor for it, Solomon forced many of the non-Israelites in the kingdom—the Amorites, Hittites, Perizzites, Hivites, and Jebusites—to work as slaves (see 1 Kings 9:20–21).

Under Solomon, Jerusalem became an urban concentration of privileged nobles and merchants who enjoyed a higher standard of living than the peasants in the villages and farms. Solomon ruled his home tribe, Judah, directly and the other tribes of Israel through administrators. As a result, the northern tribes grew resentful of the Jerusalem aristocracy.

During Solomon's moral and spiritual decline, Ahijah, a Levite prophet from Shiloh, foretold the division of Israel into northern and southern kingdoms. He also foretold that Jeroboam, one of Solomon's construction supervisors, would lead the northern kingdom:

> About that time Jeroboam was going out of Jerusalem, and Ahijah the prophet of Shiloh met him on the way, wearing a new cloak. The two of them were alone out in the country, and Ahijah took hold of the new cloak he was wearing and tore it into twelve pieces. Then he said to Jeroboam, "Take ten pieces for yourself, for this is what the LORD, the God of Israel, says: 'See, I am going to tear the kingdom out of Solomon's hand and give you ten tribes. But for the sake of My servant David and the city of Jerusalem, which I have chosen out of all the tribes of Israel, he will have one tribe. I will do this because they have forsaken Me and worshiped Ashtoreth the goddess of the Sidonians, Chemosh the god of the Moabites, and Molek the god of the Ammonites, and have not walked in obedience to me, nor done what is right in My eyes, nor kept My decrees and laws as David, Solomon's father, did.
>
> "'But I will not take the whole kingdom out of Solomon's hand; I have made him ruler all the days of his life for the sake of David My servant, whom I chose and who obeyed My commands and decrees.'"
> (1 Kings 11:29–34)

After Solomon died, the ten northern Israelite tribes revolted against his successor, Rehoboam. The united monarchy of Israel split into two kingdoms, Israel in the north and Judah (with Jerusalem) in the south. The two Jewish nations were in a state of war for decades afterwards. Around 720 BC, the northern kingdom of Israel was conquered by the Assyrian Empire and many Israelites were taken into captivity.

From about 598 BC to about 587 BC, the army of the Babylonian king, Nebuchadnezzar, laid a series of sieges to Jerusalem, resulting in the destruction of Solomon's Temple and the city walls. During those years, and as late as 582 BC, the Babylonians took thousands of Israelites into captivity and slavery.

As Jerusalem and its Temple lay in ruins, the people must have despaired. How could this have happened? God had promised King David, "Your house and your kingdom will endure forever before me; your throne will be established forever" (2 Samuel 7:16).

And God had also promised that a future king would "reign on David's throne and over his kingdom, establishing and upholding it with justice and righteousness from that time on and forever" (Isaiah 9:7). Now the throne of David was destroyed and Jerusalem was nothing but rubble. Had God's promises failed?

Amid the desolation of the northern and southern kingdoms, the people must have thought that God's Kingdom was finished, His promises could never be fulfilled. The seemingly invincible empire of Israel was laid to waste.

The Promise of an Eternal Kingdom

But even in the humiliating Babylonian captivity, there was one faithful prophet who still believed in the Kingdom of God. That prophet, Daniel, told King Nebuchadnezzar, "In the time of those kings, the God of heaven will set up a kingdom that will never be destroyed, nor will it be left to another people. It will crush all those kingdoms and bring them to an end, but it will itself endure forever" (Daniel 2:44).

Daniel was prophesying about the Kingdom of God.

For a brief time, David's kingdom sparkled like a diamond in a gold setting. The people of Israel thought it was the Kingdom of God and would endure forever. When they read the Old Testament prophecies of a coming Messiah, they pictured a new David, a warrior-king who would restore his political nation-state and sit upon David's throne.

In Acts 1, the risen Jesus appeared to His followers, walked with them, and talked with them for forty days. The account says that, during this time, He "spoke about the kingdom of God" (v. 3). On one occasion, the disciples gathered around Him and asked, "Lord, are you at this time going to restore the kingdom to Israel?" (v. 6).

After walking with Him for three years, hearing Him teach about the Kingdom, and witnessing His death and resurrection, the disciples were still locked into the Old Testament way of thinking about the Kingdom. They were still looking for a revived political kingdom with Jesus upon the throne. They didn't realize that the Kingdom of God was already among them. David's kingdom *foreshadowed* the Kingdom of God, but it was not the true and everlasting Kingdom founded and ruled by King Jesus.

Jesus replied,

> "It is not for you to know the times or dates the Father
> has set by His own authority. But you will receive power
> when the Holy Spirit comes on you; and you will be My

> witnesses in Jerusalem, and in all Judea and Samaria,
> and to the ends of the earth." (vv. 7–8)

And the moment He finished speaking, He was taken up out of their sight.

Now, as then, there is a temptation to mistake worldly political power structures for the Kingdom of God. When God told Abraham, "I will make of you a great nation" (Genesis 12:2) and "Look up at the sky and count the stars.... So shall your offspring be" (Genesis 15:5), Abraham undoubtedly thought that God was promising to create a *political* nation made up of his *physical* descendants. And Abraham was not entirely wrong—God gave him many descendants who still make up the nation of Israel.

But that promise had a much greater meaning that was hidden from view until Jesus the Messiah came among us. As the Apostle Paul wrote,

> The promises were spoken to Abraham and to his seed.
> Scripture does not say "and to seeds," meaning many
> people, but "and to your seed," meaning one person,
> who is Christ. (Galatians 3:16)

God promised Abraham a kingdom made up of *spiritual* descendants, those who believed in God's promises.

Abraham must have had an inkling that God's promise extended far beyond any geographical boundaries or political divisions. As the book of Hebrews tells us, he "was looking forward to the city with foundations, whose architect and builder is God" (Hebrews 11:10).

That city is among us now. The Kingdom of God is within all of us who follow Jesus and who are indwelt by the Spirit of God.

PART III

The Wisdom of the Kingdom

The wisdom books of the Old Testament are Job, Psalms, Proverbs, Ecclesiastes, and Song of Solomon. They consist of sayings, dialogues, and poetry. These books focus on how to live a virtuous and rewarding life amid trials, temptations, and pressures. Because true wisdom comes from and points to God, the themes of the Kingdom of God and His New Covenant can be found throughout the wisdom books.

7

Job's Kingdom Faith: Accepting God's Sovereignty

The book of Job is the first of the wisdom books in the Old Testament. (The other wisdom books are Psalms, Proverbs, Ecclesiastes, and Song of Solomon.) Job addresses the oldest, most troubling question in the Bible: Why does God allow the innocent to suffer?

In theology, the study of the problem of evil, suffering, and injustice—and the vindication of God from blame for those evils—is called *theodicy* (from the Greek words *theos* and *dikē*, meaning "God on trial"). The book of Job squarely addresses the questions of theodicy through the sufferings of the story's hero.

In a perfect world, sin and injustice should be punished and righteousness should be rewarded. But we know all too well that in the *real* world, the righteous often suffer and the wicked often prosper. Why does God allow such a moral imbalance?

A Glimpse of the Courts of Heaven

The book opens with these words: "In the land of Uz there lived a man whose name was Job. This man was blameless and upright; he feared God and shunned evil." It goes on to tell us that Job had a large family and great wealth. He was a righteous man, and he was very blessed.

The scene soon shifts to the courts of Heaven, where we see God and His angels. Then comes the adversary, Satan, the malicious fallen angel, who states that he has been roaming the earth. God asks Satan if he has noticed His righteous servant Job.

Satan replies,

> "Does Job fear God for nothing?...You have blessed the work of his hands, so that his flocks and herds are spread throughout the land. But now stretch out your hand and strike everything he has, and he will surely curse you to your face." (Job 1:9–11)

God permits Satan to afflict Job by taking away his herds, servants, and even his sons and daughters. Job goes into mourning—but he does not curse God as Satan predicted. Instead, he worships God, saying:

> "Naked I came from my mother's womb, and naked I will depart. The LORD gave and the LORD has taken away; may the name of the LORD be praised." (Job 1:21)

Amid all his sufferings, Job did not sin by accusing God of wrongdoing.

So Satan asks God for permission to afflict Job in his body and his health, saying that out of his physical pain Job would "surely curse you to your face" (Job 2:4). God grants permission, so long as Satan spares Job's life.

So Satan inflicted painful sores on Job, prompting his wife to urge him to "curse God and die" (Job 2:9). Job replied, "You are talking like a foolish woman. Shall we accept good from God, and not trouble?" In this response, the Scriptures tell us, "Job did not sin in what he said" (Job 2:10).

Miserable Comforters

Then Job's three friends appear on the scene: Eliphaz the Temanite, Bildad the Shuhite, and Zophar the Naamathite. These three men mourned with Job for seven days and seven nights. No one spoke because they saw how great Job's suffering was.

Job then delivers a monologue, cursing the day of his birth and longing for death—but death does not come. This begins a cycle of dialogues between Job and his three friends—and as they continue, the friends become Job's tormentors. They accuse Job of committing unconfessed sins. They tell him his suffering is deserved. Job angrily defends himself and replies, "You are miserable comforters, all of you! Will your long-winded speeches never end?" (Job 16:2–3).

In these debates, we see that human nature never changes. Even in the twenty-first century, when Christians suffer calamities, setbacks, or illnesses, there are still those who will act the part of "Job's comforters," offering arguments or platitudes instead of genuine empathy. There are always people who think they have all the answers for the fix you're in. They may even accuse you of hidden sin.

But neither Job's "friends" nor Job himself had all the answers for Job's suffering. God permitted Satan to act—but it was Satan who directly afflicted Job. It's important that neither Job nor his "friends" ever mentions Satan. In fact, he is only mentioned in the first two chapters. Job and his friends had a lengthy debate about the nature and causes of evil, and never once mentioned the source of evil, Satan himself.

One of the lessons of Job is that we can debate the problem of evil for days or years, but if we do not understand the great contest between good and evil, between God and Satan, then we simply don't know what we're talking about. The real struggle against evil is not taking place in the earthly realm, but in the heavenly realm—the realm we glimpse briefly in the first two chapters of Job.

God knows something that you and I tend to forget: There is no victory without battles. Or, as we sometimes hear: No pain, no gain. You will never rejoice in victory if you never suffer the pain of defeat. You will never truly empathize with a suffering person until you've suffered yourself. You will never really know what prayer is about until you have gone through the fiery furnace.

God's goal for His children is spiritual maturity. We will one day reign and rule with Him over entire planets. So in this life, we have struggles and sufferings to prepare us to reign with Him in the next life.

Job and the Kingdom of God

Job lived in a land called Uz. We don't know where Uz was located or when Job lived, but he was not an Israelite. He probably lived in the time before Abraham, so he was not a citizen of any kingdom as far as we know. As we see throughout the account, Job viewed God as his King. During his ordeals, Job grappled with the sovereign rule of God over his life, demonstrating his unwavering faith in God's sovereign kingship over him through his speeches.

Job longs for a personal audience with his sovereign King. He acknowledges God's superiority. He recognizes that God is no mere mortal, and that as a human being he cannot stand before God and make his case. In a prophetic moment, Job wishes he had a go-between to mediate between himself and God:

> "He is not a mere mortal like me that I might answer Him, that we might confront each other in court. If only there were someone to mediate between us, someone to bring us together, someone to remove God's rod from me, so that His terror would frighten me no more. Then I would speak up without fear of Him, but as it now stands with me, I cannot." (Job 9:32–35)

Here, stated obliquely but clearly, is another prophecy of the coming Messiah, who would one day serve as a mediator between God and humanity—or, as Job put it, "Someone to bring us together." As the Apostle Paul wrote centuries later, "For there is one God and one mediator between God and mankind, the man Christ Jesus" (1 Timothy 2:5).

In Job 28, Job affirms his belief in God's righteous wisdom:

> Where then does wisdom come from?
> Where does understanding dwell?...
> God understands the way to it

> and He alone knows where it dwells....
> And He said to the human race,
> "The fear of the Lord—
> that is wisdom,
> and to shun evil is understanding." (Job 28:20, 23, 28)

Throughout the book, Job maintains an attitude of submission to the kingship of God and trust in His wisdom and righteousness. Job never loses faith in God's sovereign justice.

"My Redeemer Lives"

Job went through far more pain and suffering than you and I are ever likely to know. Satan was against him, Job's circumstances were against him, and his friends were against him. Even his wife told him to curse God and die. But Job persevered with God. Because of his faithfulness, God honored him and not only restored everything Job had lost, but doubled it.

Whatever your sufferings, persevere with God. Have faith that He is working behind the scenes of your life to restore you and lead you safely into His Kingdom. Look forward to that glorious day when He will reveal everything to you that is now a mystery.

Meanwhile, we should never treat anyone's pain lightly. Everyone asks Job-like questions at some point. We must treat the painful questioning of suffering people with respect.

At the same time, we should let go of the notion that God owes us an explanation. God speaks to Job from a whirlwind, contrasting his limited understanding with His own omnipotence and wisdom. God does not defend Himself. He does not answer

Job's questions or explain Job's sufferings. Instead, He says, "Where were you when I laid the earth's foundation? Tell me, if you understand" (Job 38:4).

Some people find this response frustrating. But I submit to you that it is fitting and right that God chooses not to answer all our questions in this life. To be candid, I would refuse to worship a God who was so weak that He had to explain Himself to me. That is what Heaven is for. One day, all our questions will be answered. But for now, as Paul says, we see through a glass darkly.

There is a fascinating passage in Job 19 that every believer should know. There are some who claim that people in Old Testament times had no concept of an afterlife, and that the idea of Heaven was invented or borrowed from other cultures. This is clearly not true. After all, Genesis 5:24 tells us about a righteous man named Enoch who never saw death, because God took him straight to Heaven. And 2 Kings 2:11 tells us that the prophet Elijah did not die, but God took him to Heaven in a whirlwind. And here in Job 19, Job says:

> "Oh, that my words were recorded,
> that they were written on a scroll,
> that they were inscribed with an iron tool on lead,
> or engraved in rock forever!
> I know that my Redeemer lives,
> and that in the end He will stand on the earth.
> And after my skin has been destroyed,
> yet in my flesh I will see God;
> I myself will see Him
> with my own eyes—I, and not another.
> How my heart yearns within me!" (Job 19:23–27)

Job fully expects to be resurrected in a glorified body. He antici-pates seeing God face to face. That is one of the strongest, clearest expressions of faith in Heaven you will ever read—and it comes from one of the oldest books in the Old Testament.

Job is a book of questions, not a book of answers. It is the greatest book ever written on the subject of evil, suffering, and the injustice of this life—yet God ultimately doesn't defend or explain Himself. Job's conclusion is essentially this: God created the heavens and the earth; we didn't. God understands the complexities of the moral, spiritual, and physical universe; we don't. God knows the past, present, and future; we don't.

So before you accuse Him of unfairness, remember this: God the Father laid all the punishment of sinful, wicked humanity upon our mediator, Jesus the Son. When Job said, "I know that my Redeemer lives," he was prophesying about Jesus.

We tend to feel that our sufferings are unjust, but in fact we deserve nothing but punishment for sin. It was Jesus who endured undeserved sufferings on our behalf. With His wounds we are healed. Somehow, Job seemed to glimpse that truth while he was still in the depths of his sufferings. Whatever our trials, may you and I live daily in the light of that truth.

8

Psalms:
The Songbook of the Kingdom

The book of Psalms is a collection of 150 songs originally sung
during worship in the Temple. The word "psalm" comes from
the Greek word *psalmoi*, meaning "instrumental music" (some of
the headings of the psalms indicate the musical instruments which
should be played).

The psalms are unlike English poetry. They employ a literary
device called "parallelism." You'll find that many lines in the Psalms
form a symmetrical relationship. For example, you'll see examples
of "synonymous parallelism," in which two lines express the same
thought in different words. For example, in Psalm 27, David writes:

> The LORD is my light and my salvation—
>   whom shall I fear?
> The LORD is the stronghold of my life—
>   of whom shall I be afraid? (Psalm 27:1)

Other psalms may use "antithetical parallelism," in which the two lines use opposite ideas or examples to make a strong statement:

> The lions may grow weak and hungry, but those who seek the LORD lack no good thing. (Psalm 34:10)

With that brief background in the literary structure and style of the Psalms, let's take a closer look at a few.

Psalm 2: The Psalm of the Father, Son, and Holy Spirit

The second psalm points to King Jesus and His eternal Kingdom. The psalmist writes:

> Why do the nations conspire
> and the peoples plot in vain?
> The kings of the earth rise up
> and the rulers band together
> against the LORD and against His anointed, saying,
> "Let us break their chains
> and throw off their shackles." (Psalm 2:1–3)

The first three verses speak of the coming of Jesus, the Anointed King—and the kings of the earth's defiance against His authority.

Across the world, and even in the United States (which is already a post-Christian nation, and fast becoming an anti-Christian nation), we see growing hatred toward, and persecution of, followers of the Lord Jesus Christ. According to a 2019 report by the Pew Research Center, Christians are the most persecuted religious group in the world. They are targeted for arrest, assault, murder, discrimination, and vandalism at a level not seen since the time of Nero.[1]

A thousand years before Jesus, this psalm prophesied of a worldwide conspiracy against the Lord and His followers. Yet the psalmist also tells us that the nations and the people plot in vain. There are three distinct speakers in the next eight verses. The first is God the Father:

> The One enthroned in heaven laughs;
> the Lord scoffs at them.
> He rebukes them in His anger
> and terrifies them in His wrath, saying,
> "I have installed my king
> on Zion, my holy mountain." (Psalm 2:4–6)

The kings of the earth think they can rid themselves of God—but God laughs at them. And this is not a mirthful laugh, but a laugh of derision at man's puny rebellion against God and His Son.

The next speaker is the Jesus the Messiah. He declares that God the Father has given the nations to Him as an inheritance—and He will break them because of their rebellion:

> I will proclaim the LORD's decree:
> He said to me, "You are My Son;
> today I have become your Father.
> Ask Me,
> and I will make the nations your inheritance,
> the ends of the earth your possession.

You will break them with a rod of iron;
You will dash them to pieces like pottery." (Psalm 2:7–9)

The third speaker is the Holy Spirit, who issues a warning—and an invitation:

Therefore, you kings, be wise;
be warned, you rulers of the earth.
Serve the LORD with fear
and celebrate His rule with trembling.
Kiss His son, or He will be angry
and your way will lead to your destruction,
for His wrath can flare up in a moment.
Blessed are all who take refuge in Him. (Psalm 2:10–12)

The Spirit warns the kings of the earth to serve and love the Lord—or face destruction. The Spirit invites all to take refuge in the Son. There is no condemnation toward those who are in Jesus Christ.

Psalm 2 is one of the clearest messianic prophecies in the Old Testament. It is quoted twice in the New Testament because it is fulfilled in Jesus (see Acts 13:33; Hebrews 1:5).

Psalm 8: The Majestic Lord

This psalm of King David begins and ends with this shout of praise: "Lord, our Lord, how majestic is your name in all the earth!" When the psalmist makes the same statement at the beginning and the end, you know this is the dominant theme of the psalm.

As I read the opening verses, I suspect that King David was thinking back to an incident from his boyhood:

> LORD, our Lord,
> how majestic is your name in all the earth!
> You have set your glory
> in the heavens.
> Through the praise of children and infants
> you have established a stronghold against your enemies,
> to silence the foe and the avenger. (Psalm 8:1–2)

How does praise for God from the lips of children "establish a stronghold" and silence mortal enemies? I picture David thinking back to a scene from 1 Samuel 17, when King Saul and the Israelites squared off against the Philistine army across the Valley of Elah.

A Philistine champion, a giant named Goliath, strode out, mocking God and daring Israel to risk its fate on the outcome of a duel to the death. King Saul should have accepted the challenge, but he was afraid.

So God sent David, a young shepherd boy armed only with a leather sling and five smooth stones from a nearby brook. And this mere boy stood before Goliath and gave praise to God:

> "I come against you in the name of the LORD Almighty,
> the God of the armies of Israel, whom you have defied.
> This day the LORD will deliver you into my hands, and
> I'll strike you down and cut off your head.... All those
> gathered here will know that it is not by sword or spear
> that the LORD saves; for the battle is the LORD's, and He
> will give all of you into our hands." (1 Samuel 17:45–47)

Then David, empowered by the Spirit of God, did exactly as he had promised. He whirled the sling, let the stone fly, and it buried itself in Goliath's forehead. The giant fell dead. The foe was silenced. The Philistines fled. The stronghold of Israel was established.

What giants do you face today? What enemies render you ineffective for the Kingdom? When David cut off Goliath's head, he used the giant's own sword. When you face your own giants by God's might, He'll enable you to turn the enemy's own weapons against him.

The combat between David and Goliath was a genuine historical event, but it also had great symbolic meaning. This battle symbolizes the cosmic struggle between the Lord Jesus and Satan—a struggle going back to the Garden of Eden. David the shepherd boy foreshadows Jesus, our Good Shepherd. Goliath represents Satan—and all the giants we face in life.

Satan sends giants into our lives to intimidate us and neutralize us. We can either be like King Saul, quaking in fear, paralyzed with indecision—or we can step up like David, praising God and facing our giants with faith and courage. Our shout of victory is, "The battle is the Lord's!" (I like to think that when the stone struck Goliath's forehead, David shouted, "Timber!") The battle was won before Goliath's body hit the ground.

I believe David was mentally reliving God's victory over Goliath as he penned the first two verses of Psalm 8. Then he went on to write:

> When I consider your heavens,
>   the work of your fingers,
>   the moon and the stars,

which You have set in place,
what is mankind that You are mindful of them,
human beings that You care for them?
You have made them a little lower than the angels
and crowned them with glory and honor.
You made them rulers over the works of your hands;
You put everything under their feet:
all flocks and herds,
and the animals of the wild,
the birds in the sky,
and the fish in the sea,
all that swim the paths of the seas.
LORD, our Lord,
how majestic is your name in all the earth! (Psalm 8:3–9)

David understood that God's surpassing might and majesty is the secret to victory. When you feel discouraged, fearful, or defeated, call upon the name of the Lord. David reminds us of the power and wisdom behind that name. It's the power and wisdom that set the moon and stars in place.

Step outside on a clear night and look at the moon and the Milky Way. What you will see is majestic beyond human imagination—yet it is only a faint reflection of the real glory of God. If we could glimpse, even for a brief moment, God's full glory in Heaven, we'd see how inadequate our mere words of praise are.

David also understood the sobering measurement of man. "What is mankind that You are mindful of them, human beings that You care for them?" David compares the billions of stars in the vastness of space with his own miniscule size, and he marvels that

God even notices the human race at all. Earth is an insignificant speck in the vast ocean of the cosmos.

Yet David says of us,

> "You have made them a little lower than the angels and crowned them with glory and honor. You made them rulers over the works of your hands; You put everything under their feet."

God has crowned the human race with glory by making us in His image. He has put us in charge of the earth and its living creatures.

You are significant to God. When you hurt, He hurts with you. When you achieve some task or victory in His name, He rejoices with you. When you pray, He listens—and He answers prayer. He cares for you.

Secularists take the view that human beings are nothing more than evolved anthropoid apes. The secularists would say, "Evolution has made human beings a little higher than the chimpanzees." But David does not compare humans to beasts; he recognizes that God has made us not a little higher than beasts, but "a little lower than the angels."

Beasts have bodies, but no spirits. Angels are spirits without bodies. Human beings are the only creatures in God's creation that have both bodies and spirits. We are a little lower than the heavenly beings—but we not to be confused with any category of mere beasts. In eternity, we will receive a privilege that, before now, only the angels have known—the privilege of seeing God face to face. In that day, we will fully reflect the image of God.

It's high noon for humanity, and two forces face off across the valley. On one side is the faithful remnant who follow the Lord Jesus. On the other side is the "Philistine army" of this hateful, anti-God world—our enemies and foes. The Goliaths of this dying world have challenged us to mortal combat.

It's time to call upon the powers of Heaven. It's time to humble ourselves before God in prayer. It's time to stop living with one foot in the world and one foot in Heaven. If you put your faith in Jesus, if you risk everything for His Kingdom, if you live your life in obedience to His will, then you will one day rule and reign with the King of Kings.

Lord Jesus, how majestic is Your name in all the earth!

Psalm 24: The King of Glory

The Ark of the Covenant was the most sacred object in ancient Israel. It was an acacia wood chest covered in gold with an ornately carved lid called the Mercy Seat. It contained the two stone tablets of the Ten Commandments. God gave Moses the pattern of the Ark at the foot of Mount Sinai. When the Israelites traveled, the Levites used long wooden poles to carry it. It represented the presence of God in the midst of His people, and it was a symbol of the Israelites' national identity.

In the days before they had a king, the Israelites fought the Philistines at Ebenezer. The Philistines won, killing four thousand Israelite soldiers.

Confused and discouraged, the Israelites decided to trust a sacred object, rather than God alone, to give them the victory. With the Ark in their camp, the Israelites went onto the battlefield—and their defeat was worse than before. The Philistines killed thirty thousand Israelites and captured the Ark of the Covenant. With the loss of the Ark, many in Israel concluded, "The Glory has departed from Israel" (1 Samuel 4:21).

The Philistines thought they had captured Israel's "good-luck charm," but wherever they took the Ark, disaster befell them. The Philistines placed it in the temple of their god Dagon—and they soon found their idol lying prostrate before the Ark. The Philistines were besieged by plagues, tumors, and rats. The Ark had brought the Philistines death and a curse. Seven months after capturing it, the Philistines were desperate to give it back to the Israelites.

The Israelites gladly received the Ark, along with the "guilt offerings" of gold the Philistines offered. The Ark was kept for a while in the field of Joshua the Beth-Shemite, and it was later moved to Kirjath-jearim, where it remained for twenty years. The Ark was largely ignored during King Saul's reign (see 1 Chronicles 13:3).

But at the beginning of King David's reign, he had the Ark moved from Kirjath-Jearim to Mount Zion in Jerusalem. But he failed to have the Ark transported on poles by Levites, as the Law required. Instead, the Ark was placed on a cart. When the cart hit a bump, a man tried to steady the Ark with his hand—and God struck him dead for touching it.

So David sent Levites to bring the Ark to Mount Zion on poles, as God had commanded. As it approached Jerusalem, the Bible tells us, "David was dancing before the LORD with all his might, while he and all Israel were bringing up the Ark of the LORD with shouts and the sound of trumpets" (2 Samuel 6:14–15).

The Ark was once more in the midst of the Israelites, in the city that King David had made his capital. It was an emotional

reunion between the Ark and the Israelites, and David received it
with unrestrained, exuberant dancing.

Many Bible scholars believe that David composed Psalm 24 as
a hymn of praise to God for the Ark's return.

> The earth is the LORD's, and everything in it,
> the world, and all who live in it;
> for He founded it on the seas
> and established it on the waters.
> Who may ascend the mountain of the LORD?
> Who may stand in His holy place?
> The one who has clean hands and a pure heart,
> who does not trust in an idol
> or swear by a false god.
> They will receive blessing from the LORD
> and vindication from God their Savior.
> Such is the generation of those who seek Him,
> who seek your face, God of Jacob.
> Lift up your heads, you gates;
> be lifted up, you ancient doors,
> that the King of glory may come in.
> Who is this King of glory?
> The LORD strong and mighty,
> the LORD mighty in battle.
> Lift up your heads, you gates;
> lift them up, you ancient doors,
> that the King of glory may come in.
> Who is He, this King of glory?
> The LORD Almighty—
> He is the King of glory. (Psalm 24:1–10)

After David brought the Ark to Jerusalem, he wanted to build a great temple to honor God's Name and house the Ark. But God told him, "You are not to build a house for My Name, because you are a warrior and have shed blood" (1 Chronicles 28:3). The Temple was later built by David's son Solomon.

As the priests of the Temple designed liturgies for the days of the calendar, they designated Psalm 24 as the psalm for the first day of the week—that is, Sunday. So, when Jesus entered Jerusalem in triumph on the first Palm Sunday, Psalm 24 was the song of the day. The priests and the choir were singing this song in the Temple on the day the Messiah was presented to Israel as the King of Kings.

Also, on Easter Sunday—the very day the Lord Jesus conquered death and strode triumphantly from the tomb—the Temple choir was getting ready to sing Psalm 24. So you can appreciate the power of this song of lofty praise.

The first two verses tell us that God owns the universe. You might say, "But doesn't the Bible tell us that Satan is the prince of this world?" Paul in Ephesians 2:2 rightly calls Satan "the ruler of the kingdom of the air, the spirit who is now at work in those who are disobedient."

But the Lord claims ownership of His *entire* creation—the billions of galaxies with their countless stars and planets, the vast realms of space with their unfathomable orbits. They all belong to Him—including Planet Earth.

And yet, Satan is undeniably the prince of this world. How could God own the earth while he is its prince? The answer is found in the story of the fall of Satan—and the fall of humanity. Satan was once a great angel. His name (from the Latin Vulgate edition of the Old Testament) was "Lucifer," which means "light-bringer" or "morning star." The prophet Isaiah describes his fall:

> How you have fallen from heaven,
> morning star, son of the dawn!
> You have been cast down to the earth,
> you who once laid low the nations! (Isaiah 14:12)

Afterward, Lucifer wanted to take the earth for his domain—but he couldn't because God had given Adam dominion over it. So Lucifer hatched a plan: He would tempt Adam to sin, cause him to fall, and in so doing hand his dominion of Earth to Satan on a silver platter.

God had to reinstate His authority over Earth—and He did so by sending His Son as the New Adam to rescue us (and by extension, the earth) from the adversary. The battle that reinstated God's authority over the earth took place on a hill called Calvary.

The earth is the Lord's, and everything in it, no matter what atheists, secularists, and radical environmentalists say. The earth is not a pagan goddess named Gaia. It is a masterpiece of God's creation, as are all who live in it.

Satan still roams the earth, causing destruction, suffering, and wickedness. But Satan's legal claim was canceled on the cross. Now he is nothing but an imposter and a pretender whose time on earth is growing shorter every day.

Psalm 24 contains God's ultimate offer to the human race. It begins with a question: "Who may ascend the mountain of the Lord? Who may stand in His holy place?" Without God's forgiving grace, the only conceivable answer is: "No one." No human being ever born, except Jesus, is sinless—and only the righteous may stand in God's holy place.

Verse 4 tells us that the only one who may ascend the mountain of the Lord is "one who has clean hands and a pure heart." In

David's day, only the high priest could enter the Holy of Holies—and only once a year, for a brief time. And when he was there, he trembled with dread and awe.

But verse 5 contains a prophecy and an invitation. The Lord is issuing an all-inclusive invitation to everyone, flinging open the door of Heaven. Those with clean hands and pure hearts, David writes, "will receive blessing from the Lord and vindication from God their Savior."

Now, the fact is that you and I do not have clean hands or pure hearts. We are sinners, children of Adam and Eve. But by faith we have been cleansed by the blood of Jesus, and by God's grace we have been vindicated and justified. Only through His grace and the sacrifice of Jesus can we have clean hands and a pure heart. And we can only receive God's forgiving grace by loving God, not the world; by living for God, not the self. That is what it means to live by faith.

When we accept God's ultimate offer and receive the blessing and vindication of the Lord, we are adopted into His family. The Father of our Lord and Savior is now our Father—the One who owns the universe.

In the final verses of Psalm 24, we see that the Lord's victory is inevitable. God cannot lose. Satan cannot win. The Lord is strong and mighty in battle. That is the triumphant message of verses 7 through 10.

There may be war in the Middle East. Russia and China may invade their neighbors. There may be terrorist attacks in the United States. No matter what sorts of evil human beings inflict on one another, the Lord will overcome.

Five times in the last three verses of Psalm 24, David exalts Christ as the King of Glory. We have been brainwashed to believe Jesus is meek and lowly. Many people confuse meekness with weakness. Jesus was meek—but He was anything but weak. He came and preached the good news of the Kingdom of God. He Himself is our victorious Lord, our conquering King of glory.

Our God is a conquering God. He has defeated Satan and sin. He has overcome the grave. He is the Lord, strong and mighty in battle! And we, as members of His Church, have been called to conquer in His Name. The church that is not conquering and taking territory and winning souls is not the church of Jesus Christ.

Verse 9 refers to the Ark of the Covenant entering Jerusalem: "Lift up your heads, you gates; lift them up, you ancient doors, that the King of glory may come in." The Ark represented the glorious presence of God, passing through the doors of the city and coming to rest among His people.

Yet we may also apply this imagery to the Lord entering our lives. The image of the King of Glory entering through the doors of the city is reminiscent of the imagery of Revelation 3:20, where Jesus says,

> "Here I am! I stand at the door and knock. If anyone hears My voice and opens the door, I will come in and eat with that person, and they with Me."

If you have never invited the King of Glory into your life, today is the day, now is the time. Open the door of your heart and let Him occupy your life.

Psalm 93: The King and His Kingdom

I have lived under a dictatorship, under socialism, and under oppression. After Gamal Abdel Nasser led the Egyptian revolution of 1952, Egypt, the land where I was born, was ruled by a dictator who cultivated a cult of personality. In fact, Nasser popularized the authoritarian model of regimes now widely practiced in Arab nations. I didn't choose the government under which I was raised.

But God has given us a privilege—the right to choose to be ruled by the Jesus the King. Let's look at Psalm 93:

> The LORD reigns, He is robed in majesty;
>   the LORD is robed in majesty and armed with strength;
>   indeed, the world is established, firm and secure.
> Your throne was established long ago;
>   You are from all eternity.
> The seas have lifted up, LORD,
>   the seas have lifted up their voice;
>   the seas have lifted up their pounding waves.
> Mightier than the thunder of the great waters,
>   mightier than the breakers of the sea—
>   the LORD on high is mighty.
> Your statutes, LORD, stand firm;
>   holiness adorns your house
>   for endless days. (Psalm 93:1–5)

Psalm 93 declares the kingship of Yahweh. The psalmist tells us that God is exalted in three ways. First, He is exalted by the triumph of His reign. The psalmist tells us, "The Lord reigns, He is robed in majesty." God reigns over all the earth, whether we, the atheists, or the tyrants of the world like it or not.

At Christmastime, we like to think of Jesus as a helpless baby lying in a manger. But He did not remain a baby. He was nailed to a cross like a common criminal. He was mocked and bled to death for our sins. But now He is enthroned over the entire universe. He is robed in majesty, and all power and authority belong to Him.

When John saw the majesty of the Lord, he fell on his face in worship (Revelation 1:17). When Isaiah saw the Lord's splendor, he cried,

> "I am ruined! For I am a man of unclean lips, and I live among a people of unclean lips, and my eyes have seen the King, the LORD Almighty." (Isaiah 6:5)

Most of us go about our lives full of our own self-importance, eager to take credit for what God has done. But when we catch even a faint glimpse of the absolute splendor and might of the Lord, we realize that we are ruined and unclean. We are forced to step down from the throne of our lives, to fall on our faces before Him, and confess, "The Lord reigns, He is robed in majesty!"

Second, God is exalted over all who oppose His authority. The psalmist writes, "The seas have lifted up," but "mightier than the breakers of the sea—the Lord on high is mighty."

The Scriptures often depict the enemies of God as fierce ocean waves. Isaiah wrote:

> Woe to the many nations that rage—
> they rage like the raging sea!
> Woe to the peoples who roar—
> they roar like the roaring of great waters! (Isaiah 17:12)

The prophet Jeremiah also depicts God's enemies as a raging sea:

> They are armed with bow and spear;
> they are cruel and show no mercy.
> They sound like the roaring sea
> as they ride on their horses. (Jeremiah 6:23)

Like these two prophets, the psalmist gives us a vivid image of those who reject the authority of God's Word and His authority over their lives: "The seas have lifted up their voice; the seas have lifted up their pounding waves." The mass of godless humanity is a churning, pounding wave. It raises its collective voice in defiance against God.

You see many godless people on television, smiling pleasantly as they ceaselessly mock God and all those who follow Him. They have rejected the authority of Jesus over their lives, just as they have rejected His salvation. They refuse to acknowledge the sovereign supremacy of the King of Kings. They are like the roaring of the ocean—loud, ceaseless, and mindless.

Those who belong to Jesus will live with Him forever. Those who reject and rage against Him will continue to pound the shore. But the Lord is mightier than the breakers of the sea.

Third, God is exalted by the truth of His rule. Verse 5 tells us that His perfect laws "stand firm." And, the psalmist adds, "holiness adorns your house for endless days."

There has never been a time in history when there was such a clear choice between the rule of God and the rule of Satan. Here's what you need to know about dictators: They don't give you any choices. They tell you what to do, and if you don't do it, they punish you. Satan is the cruelest dictator who ever existed. If you let him, Satan will enslave you. He will take away your power to choose. He might enslave you through a lust for power, wealth, or status.

He might enslave you through addiction to drugs, alcohol, tobacco, gambling, spending, pornography, adultery, or profanity. But if you give him one inch of your life, he will take a mile. He will control you 100 percent.

The psalmist wants you to know that God has given you the power to live as a free human being under the pleasant and gracious rule of Jesus the King. You don't have to remain in bondage under the dictatorship of Satan.

The statutes and laws of the Kingdom stand firm. Holiness adorns the house of the Lord. Holiness means surrendering to the God who loves you. Once you have surrendered fully to Him, you will live in the house of the Lord for endless days.

9

Wisdom of the Kingdom:
The Books of Solomon

Rosalind Picard is one of the leading researchers in the field of artificial intelligence. The founder of the Affective Computing Research Group at the Massachusetts Institute of Technology, she designs AI systems to solve health problems.

Raised in a family that never attended church or even mentioned religion, Rosalind said she viewed Christians as people who had "thrown their brains out the window."[1] As a teenager, she babysat for a Christian doctor and his wife while they attended Bible studies. She couldn't understand why they wasted time studying the Bible.

When that couple invited Rosalind to attend church with them, she pretended to be ill. When they asked her the following week, she claimed to be sick again.

"Faking sickness to a doctor really wasn't working," she recalled.

> They asked if I'd read the Bible. I was a straight-A student—
> one of those obnoxious kids who thought myself really

smart. So, I thought I should probably read the bestselling book of all time. I agreed to take their advice to read the book of Proverbs, one a day for a month. I saw there was all this wisdom...stuff I could learn from. I was humbled. Then I set out to read the whole Bible. And that changed me.[2]

What makes these Old Testament proverbs so powerful? There can only be one answer: The wisdom of Proverbs comes from God Himself.

Proverbs: God's Roadmap to Wisdom

The book of Proverbs is the owner's manual for the human life. If you want a rewarding, meaningful, satisfying life, then you need to spend serious time in Proverbs. The first twenty-nine chapters were written by King Solomon. Chapter 30 is credited to an unknown man, Agur son of Jakeh. Chapter 31 is described as "The sayings of King Lemuel—an inspired utterance his mother taught him."

King Solomon reigned for forty years at the height of Israel's Golden Age, and was renowned for his wisdom, which is proven by the great success of his kingdom. We can explore his wisdom in the three books he wrote, Proverbs, Ecclesiastes, and Song of Solomon.

How did Solomon become so wise? Soon after being anointed king of Israel, he made sacrifices to God on the hilltop altar at Gibeon. During the night, God appeared to him in a dream, saying, "Ask for whatever you want Me to give you."

Solomon replied, "Give your servant a discerning heart to govern your people and to distinguish between right and wrong. For who is able to govern this great people of yours?"

God was pleased with Solomon's prayer and said,

> "Since you have asked for this and not for long life or
> wealth for yourself, nor have asked for the death of your
> enemies but for discernment in administering justice,
> I will do what you have asked. I will give you a wise
> and discerning heart, so that there will never have been
> anyone like you, nor will there ever be. Moreover, I will
> give you what you have not asked for—both wealth and
> honor—so that in your lifetime you will have no equal
> among kings." (1 Kings 3:11–13)

When you read the Proverbs of Solomon, you are exploring God's
answer to his prayer for wisdom. The purpose of Proverbs is to provide
the reader with a guide to effective living and wise decision-making:

> The proverbs of Solomon son of David, king of Israel:
> for gaining wisdom and instruction;
> for understanding words of insight;
> for receiving instruction in prudent behavior,
> doing what is right and just and fair;
> for giving prudence to those who are simple,
> knowledge and discretion to the young—
> let the wise listen and add to their learning,
> and let the discerning get guidance—
> for understanding proverbs and parables,
> the sayings and riddles of the wise. (Proverbs 1:1–6)

The next verse gives us the key to unlocking the wisdom of
this book:

> The fear of the LORD is the beginning of knowledge,
> but fools despise wisdom and instruction. (Proverbs 1:7)

If you want to be wise, you must first understand that all wisdom begins with an attitude the Bible calls "the fear of the Lord." Does this mean we should cower in terror before God? Of course not. But we must approach Him with reverent awe and with an absolute submission to His will. That is the beginning of wisdom.

The first seven chapters of Proverbs are discourses on wisdom from a wise father to his son. These chapters address such issues as the importance of seeking wisdom from the Lord, avoiding temptation and envy, choosing friends wisely, standing firm against peer pressure, and maintaining pure speech. This discourse is summarized in these key verses:

> Trust in the LORD with all your heart
> and lean not on your own understanding;
> in all your ways submit to Him,
> and He will make your paths straight. (Proverbs 3:5–6)

Chapters 8 and 9 personify wisdom as a woman who says, "To you, O people, I call out; I raise my voice to all mankind....I open my lips to speak what is right" (Proverbs 8:4, 6). In these chapters, Lady Wisdom contrasts two ways of life—the rewarding way of the wise and the self-destructive path of the foolish.

Chapters 10 to 22 contain nuggets of wisdom from King Solomon himself. There is so much godly insight and advice that I could write encyclopedia-length volumes about them and still not do them justice. Let's look just at three verses in this section:

The name of the LORD is a fortified tower;
the righteous run to it and are safe.
The wealth of the rich is their fortified city;
they imagine it a wall too high to scale.
(Proverbs 18:10–11)

These two verses provide a stark contrast between those who take refuge in the Lord for peace and security and those who hide behind flimsy walls of wealth. In today's uncertain world, we are surrounded by voices, shouting at us: "Buy gold!" "Buy silver!" "The stock market is plunging!" "War in the Middle East!" "War in Europe!" "War in Asia!" I want to you to know that whenever you hear that the world around you is crumbling, or whenever you feel your own world is caving in on you, the Name of the Lord is a strong tower.

The Bible has revealed to us many names of God, and each reveals a unique and comforting facet of His character: *Jehovah Jireh*, "the Lord our Provider"; *Jehovah Rapha*, "the Lord our Healer"; *Jehovah Nissi*, "the Lord our Banner"; *Jehovah Shalom*, "the Lord our Peace"; *Jehovah Raah*, "the Lord our Shepherd"; and on and on, name after name. And each of these names is a strong, fortified, unscalable tower of refuge for us.

Proverbs: Kingdom and Covenant Themes

Beginning with Proverbs 22:17, Solomon records a series of "sayings of the wise" on several subjects: do not oppress the needy, avoid hot-tempered people, don't overextend yourself with debt, be diligent and skilled in your work, avoid the trap of power and greed, and so forth—advice as timely today as it was three thousand years ago.

Proverbs 25 through 29 contain sayings of Solomon collected by the officials of Hezekiah, king of Judah.

Though it may not be obvious, the themes of the Kingdom of God and His New Covenant with humanity are woven throughout this book. Proverbs is all about living according to the precepts and principles of the Kingdom of God. It instructs us in such Kingdom values as wisdom, justice, integrity, and righteous living.

For example, Proverbs 14:34 sets forth this Kingdom principle: "Righteousness exalts a nation, but sin condemns any people." And Proverbs 16:11 reminds us: "Honest scales and balances belong to the LORD; all the weights in the bag are of his making."

The New Covenant theme in Proverbs can be found in verses that emphasize God's love, grace, and forgiveness. For example, Solomon tells us, "Through love and faithfulness sin is atoned for; through the fear of the LORD evil is avoided" (Proverbs 16:6). And he says, "Whoever conceals their sins does not prosper, but the one who confesses and renounces them finds mercy" (Proverbs 28:13). This Old Testament wisdom resonates with the New Testament assurance of 1 John 1:9: "If we confess our sins, He is faithful and just and will forgive us our sins and purify us from all unrighteousness."

Proverbs 30 contains the proverbs of the unknown writer Agur, who writes in a distinctly different style from Solomon. Here is one of my favorite passages from this chapter:

> "Two things I ask of you, LORD;
>   do not refuse me before I die:
> Keep falsehood and lies far from me;
>   give me neither poverty nor riches,

but give me only my daily bread.
Otherwise, I may have too much and disown you
and say, 'Who is the LORD?'
Or I may become poor and steal,
and so dishonor the name of my God."
(Proverbs 30:7–9)

Chapter 31 is called "The sayings of King Lemuel—an inspired utterance his mother taught him." There is no mention of a king named Lemuel in the Bible or in secular history. The meaning of the name is uncertain, though some Hebrew scholars believe it could mean "belonging to God." Some have suggested that "Lemuel" was a term of endearment that Solomon's mother, Bathsheba, affectionately gave him. Because of the style of the writing and because no "King Lemuel" is known to history, many Bible scholars believe that Lemuel was a pseudonym for Solomon. I agree with this view.

She says, "Listen, son of my womb! Listen, my son, the answer to my prayers!" In other words, this mother calls her son an answer to her prayers, suggesting the special spiritual relationship she has with both God and her son. She then gives him a series of instructions and warnings against promiscuity, drunkenness, and ruling unjustly and oppressively.

In Proverbs 31:10–31, the writer draws a clear word-picture of what the Jews call the *Eshet ḥayil* or "woman of valor." I like to think of this woman as the "marvelous mom."

I have a theory that Solomon may have composed this section late in life, after he made the mistake of marrying many princesses of other nations in order to form political alliances. The result was that these princesses brought their own pagan idols and beliefs into the marriages—and Solomon compromised his faithfulness to God by permitting and participating in idolatry.

Perhaps Solomon, in his remorse over his sins and failings, remembered the sterling example of his great-great-grandmother, Ruth. As Boaz said to Ruth, "All the people of my town know that you are a woman of noble character" (Ruth 3:11). I think it is more than coincidental that Boaz's description of Ruth— "a woman of noble character"—is echoed in Proverbs 31:10: "A wife of noble character who can find? She is worth far more than rubies."

The book of Ruth tells us that Solomon's great-great-grand-mother was a Gentile (a non-Jew) from the land of Moab, yet she had rejected the false gods of the Moabites and had fed upon the godly teaching of her Israelite mother-in-law, Naomi. Ruth obeyed the God of Israel, and she became part of the lineage of King David, Solomon, and the Lord Jesus Christ.

Verses 11 to 27 describe such a woman as being hard-working, dependable, wise in money and real estate matters—a woman who "lacks nothing of value." She diligently looks after her family's material, physical, emotional, and spiritual needs. She is respected in the community (v. 23). She is generous to the poor (v. 20).

A virtuous woman earns the praise of her husband and children (vv. 28–29). To be a woman of virtue is infinitely more honorable than to be charming or beautiful (vv. 30–31).

I was raised by a Proverbs 31 marvelous mom. As I was growing up, I watched her give generously of herself, not only to our family but also to neighbors and strangers. Yet she never permitted anyone to praise her or talk about her good deeds. She was looking forward to a "Well done, faithful servant!" from her Lord and Savior, and had no desire for the praise of people.

I'll never forget the day of her funeral. The pastor who preached was well aware of the good works she had done in secret—and he had honored her wishes and kept her secrets. But at her funeral, he said, "A very expensive bottle of perfume has been broken. And all of us can experience its beautiful fragrance. All those years, she permitted no one to speak of her unselfish giving. But now that she's in Heaven, we can speak freely of her acts of kindness and mercy."

The book of Proverbs is a great edifice constructed of godly, practical wisdom. The capstone of this edifice is a beautiful word-picture of a wise, virtuous woman. A woman who fears the Lord is a role model for every believer.

Ecclesiastes: Everything under the Sun

The book of Ecclesiastes has had a profound impact on our musical culture. In the 1950s, folk singer Pete Seeger penned a song called "Turn! Turn! Turn!" which became a rock anthem for the 1960s counterculture; it is based on a passage from this book. Likewise, the song "Dust in the Wind" by the rock band Kansas is a meditation on Ecclesiastes 1:14 ("all the things that are done under the sun...are meaningless, a chasing after the wind") and 3:20 ("all come from dust, and to dust all return"). And Coldplay's "Viva la Vida" is a song about a king who "used to rule the world" but as he hears the ringing of "Jerusalem bells," he reflects on the brevity and emptiness of a life built on "pillars of sand." It sounds much like Solomon's musings in Ecclesiastes.

Ecclesiastes has a reputation for being full of doom and gloom, a depressing assessment of the meaninglessness of life. And while it often expresses a sense of existential bleakness, much of the book is inspiring, hopeful, and uplifting.

For example, Ecclesiastes 3:11 tells us, "He has made everything beautiful in its time. He has also set eternity in the human heart; yet no one can fathom what God has done from beginning to end." And Ecclesiastes 9:7 encourages us to "Go, eat your food with gladness, and drink your wine with a joyful heart, for God has already approved what you do."

Ecclesiastes is not a book of despair, but wisdom. Solomon's main theme is that it is wise to face facts, acknowledge the brevity of life, and confess that—from a purely human perspective, apart from God—life is meaningless.

When Solomon was king of Israel, two women came before him so he could judge their dispute. They lived in the same house and had given birth within days of each other. One of the babies had died in the night, and each woman claimed that the living baby was her own.

King Solomon said, "Bring me a sword." When it was brought, Solomon announced his decision: The baby would be cut in half, and each woman would receive one.

One woman agreed with Solomon's decision, saying, "Neither I nor you shall have him. Cut him in two!"

But the other woman pleaded, "Please, my lord, give her the living baby! Don't kill him!"

Then Solomon ordered that the baby be given to the woman who pleaded for the baby's life. She had proven herself to be the true mother of the child.

The biblical account concludes, "When all Israel heard the verdict the king had given, they held the king in awe, because they saw that he had wisdom from God to administer justice" (see 1 Kings 3:16–28).

The Inspired Book of Error

In Ecclesiastes 7:19, Solomon tells us, "Wisdom makes one wise person more powerful than ten rulers in a city." In this world, we face many decisions involving insoluble problems. We face temptation, seduction, and deception from Satan and the sinful influences of the world. People seek to manipulate us and control our beliefs through advertising, social media, and political rhetoric.

If we want to have the power to make good decisions, think for ourselves, and keep this fallen world from squeezing us into its mold, we need wisdom from God's Word. Godly wisdom gives us power to discern Satan's traps and defeat his schemes.

From a human perspective, Solomon viewed wisdom as immensely valuable and worthy of seeking, yet beyond the reach of his intellect. He wrote:

> All this I tested by wisdom and I said,
> "I am determined to be wise"—
> but this was beyond me.
> Whatever exists is far off and most profound—
> who can discover it?
> So I turned my mind to understand,
> to investigate and to search out wisdom and the scheme
> of things
> and to understand the stupidity of wickedness
> and the madness of folly. (Ecclesiastes 7:23–25)

Solomon is writing here from the perspective of fallen humanity, not from God's infinite and omniscient perspective. He concludes that in his fallen state, wisdom is "beyond me"—unattainable. And it is true that, for a fallen human being, apart from the enlightenment of the Holy Spirit, it is. The reason Solomon seems to despair of ever finding true wisdom is that Ecclesiastes, although inspired by God, stands alone among all the books of the Bible in reflecting a purely human point of view, not the perspective of God Himself.

Ecclesiastes is frequently misquoted and misused. In fact, when I was a boy, I twisted a verse from it myself when I wanted to get out of doing my homework. I said, "Well, Mom and Dad, don't you know that all this schoolwork and study is bad for me? Ecclesiastes 1:18 says, 'For with much wisdom comes much sorrow; the more knowledge, the more grief.'" Of course, my parents replied, "The only grief you're going to get is if you don't finish your homework!"

One of my early mentors, Bible teacher Ray Stedman, called Ecclesiastes "the inspired book of error." In *Adventuring through the Bible*, he wrote:

> This book is filled with error, yet it is wholly inspired. This may confuse some people because many feel that inspiration is a guarantee of truth. This is not necessarily so. Inspiration merely guarantees accuracy from a particular point of view: If it is God's point of view, it is true; if it is a human point of view, it may or may not be true....
>
> Because Ecclesiastes reflects a human, rather than a divine, point of view, it is often misused and twisted out of context by the enemies of God's Word. Ecclesiastes is the favorite book of atheists and agnostics. Many cults love to quote this book's erroneous viewpoints and give

the impression that these are scriptural, divine words of God concerning life.

In order to come to such a conclusion, however, one has to ignore what Ecclesiastes clearly states at the outset and repeats throughout the book: It draws its conclusion from appearances, from looking at the world from a human perspective. Every aspect of life this book examines is seen as "under the sun."[3]

That phrase "under the sun" is the key to accurately interpreting the book of Ecclesiastes. It appears twenty-seven times. What does Solomon mean by "under the sun"? He is speaking specifically of life as it is experienced on the surface of the earth, "under the sun."

The book of Ecclesiastes is unflinchingly honest in its diagnosis of the human condition. That's why it seems so bleak.

The book opens with these words (in the New International Version): "The words of the Teacher, son of David, king in Jerusalem." Other translations say, "The words of the Preacher." The Message says, "These are the words of the Quester." The original Hebrew word is *qōhelet*, which means more than merely a preacher or teacher, but has the sense of a searcher or inquirer or investigator—a person who searches deeply into a matter, then comes back and reports what he has found.

The book of Ecclesiastes is the result of King Solomon's long search for meaning and truth.

"Meaningless! Meaningless!"

Some Bible scholars believe Solomon wrote this book late in life, after he began to drift away from God, lured away by the pagan gods of his foreign wives. I disagree. I think he probably wrote it in the middle of his life, when he reached that stage when people realize they have more yesterdays than tomorrows. I think he paused in the middle of life and took stock of his existence. Even though a king enjoys a luxurious lifestyle, Solomon's daily grind consisted of the same boring activities day after day—meeting with dignitaries, judging legal disputes, negotiating trade deals, or discussing tax policy with his advisors.

And what did he have to look forward to? Death. Like all men, kings are born, live, and die—and the earth and sky go on while the king's fame and achievements are soon forgotten. Out of this midlife crisis, Solomon took pen in hand and wrote the book of Ecclesiastes.

King David had warned him not to forsake his faith in the God of Israel:

> "And you, my son Solomon, acknowledge the God of
> your father, and serve Him with wholehearted devotion
> and with a willing mind, for the LORD searches every
> heart and understands every desire and every thought. If
> you seek Him, He will be found by you; but if you forsake
> Him, He will reject you forever. Consider now, for the
> LORD has chosen you to build a house as the sanctuary.
> Be strong and do the work." (1 Chronicles 28:9–10)

But when Solomon turned to other gods, he was living "under the sun," and he lost God's perspective on life.

The Law of Moses laid out God's commandments to the kings of Israel, so that they would rule wisely and righteously. Solomon failed to heed these commands from the book of Deuteronomy:

> The king, moreover, must not acquire great numbers of horses for himself or make the people return to Egypt to get more of them, for the LORD has told you, "You are not to go back that way again." He must not take many wives, or his heart will be led astray. He must not accumulate large amounts of silver and gold. (Deuteronomy 17:16–17)

Solomon sinned in all three of these commands. He accumulated horses and gold and many wives—and he purchased many horses and chariots from Egypt, where he was forbidden to send his servants. In Solomon's final years, God allowed him to be troubled by enemies, including Hadad of Edom, Rezon of Zobah, and a rebellious official of his own government, Jeroboam. And 1 Kings 11 records that the Lord punished Solomon by allowing all the tribes of Israel except Judah to rebel against Solomon's son, Rehoboam. Thus, Israel was divided into two warring kingdoms.

Take a good look at your life. Are you living under the sun—or above it? If you are wandering in the parched wasteland of Ecclesiastes, I have good news for you. You can rise above your meaningless existence. You don't have to remain under the sun.

Those who live in a personal relationship with the Son of God not only experience joy and contentment in this life, but they know that an even richer, more rewarding future awaits them in His presence. Those who have placed their trust in Jesus will one day have perfect knowledge, perfect memories, and perfect resurrection bodies. You can live above the sun because you know who you are—and whose you are. You have a meaningful life because you know your ultimate destination.

So get out from under the sun! When you gain God's perspective on life and have the mind of Christ, then you will truly live above the sun.

Song of Solomon: Honest, Pure, and Chaste

You have probably never heard of Annie Besant, but in the late 1800s and early 1900s, she was a famed socialist activist in Great Britain. She authored many books that sparked controversy in British society, including *My Path to Atheism* (1878) and *Why I Am a Socialist* (1886). In 1890, Besant met the infamous Russian mystic Helena Blavatsky.

After rejecting the God of the Bible, Besant had an emptiness in her soul that left her wide open to the fraudulent mystical claims of Madame Blavatsky and her Theosophical Society. She fell for Blavatsky's far-fetched stories of being mentored by the Masters of the Ancient Wisdom in Tibet and of experiencing miraculous supernatural phenomena. Though Blavatsky was repeatedly and credibly accused of fraud, Besant's gullible devotion to Theosophy never wavered.

Besant continued to attack the Bible. One of her books was *Is the Bible Indictable? Being an Enquiry Whether the Bible Comes within the Ruling of the Lord Chief Justice as to Obscene Literature.* Besant didn't honestly care about so-called "obscene literature." As a self-proclaimed "freethinker," she rejected the Christian church, Christian sexual ethics, and the sanctity of marriage. But she eagerly grasped at any straw to discredit God's Word.

Besant called the Song of Solomon "a marriage-song of the sensual and luxuriant character." Citing several passages, she asked,

> Could any language be more alluring, more seductive, more passion-rousing, than…this Eastern marriage-ode? It is not vulgarly coarse and offensive as is so much of the Bible, but it is, according to the ruling of the Lord Chief Justice, a very obscene poem.[4]

These are, of course, the words of an enemy of the Bible, desperate to have it banned. She slandered one of the most beautiful and unique books in God's Word. While the Song of Solomon rejoices in the romantic intimacy between a man and his wife, it does so with words and images that are God-breathed.

This book operates on at least two levels. On the surface, it expresses the yearnings of our innermost being for romantic love. It frankly explores the human experience of romantic love within the safe enclosure of marriage—an experience which has been blessed and approved by our Creator since the time of Adam and Eve.

Though the book is honest and forthright, it never debases its subject, nor does it stir unclean thoughts in the reader. Its language is poetic, and it treats romantic love through rich and meaningful metaphors and images. It is an exquisitely pure and chaste book that honestly describes how a husband and wife delight in each other's love.

A Sacred Allegory

On a deeper level, the Song of Solomon is richly allegorical and spiritual—and that is why it is sacred to both Judaism and Christianity. In the Jewish tradition, the Song of Solomon is an allegory of God's loving relationship with the people of Israel. Among

Christians, it is an allegory of the love between Jesus the Messiah and His Bride, the Church.

In 1 Kings 4:32, we learn that Solomon penned three thousand proverbs and 1,005 songs. Most of the songs Solomon wrote have been lost, but this book, inspired by the Holy Spirit, is clearly his greatest song of all—which is why, in the first verse, he calls it his "Song of Songs."

This Song of Solomon is structured as a stage musical. The New International Version helpfully underscores the structure by dividing the text with subheads, telling us who is speaking in each section: "She" (the Beloved, the Shulamite woman), "He" (Solomon, the young king of Israel), and "Friends" (the Beloved's female friends, who rejoice with her).

The play tells the story of the Shulamite, a poor but beautiful young woman who toils in the vineyards under the hot sun. One day, she sees a handsome stranger, a shepherd grazing his flocks at midday. Their eyes meet, and they are instantly attracted to each other. They fall in love, then he mysteriously departs. She dreams of him, and he eventually returns to her—and she discovers that this handsome shepherd is in fact the king of Israel.

The shepherd (the king in disguise) courts the Shulamite in Song of Solomon 1:1–3:5. The king and the Shulamite wed in Song of Solomon 3:6–5:1. We see them work through the adjustments of young married life in Song of Solomon 5:2–7:10. In the final section, Song of Solomon 7:11–7:14, the king and his beloved journey to the home where she was raised and their love deepens.

Three times, the Shulamite woman gives a word of godly moral advice to the "daughters of Jerusalem"—by which she means all unmarried women. She says, "Do not arouse or awaken love until it so desires" (Song of Solomon 2:7; 3:5; 8:4).

When does love desire to be aroused and awakened? When it is in the safe enclosure of a marriage covenant. First, a man and woman must experience attraction, then the budding of love, then they must enter into a covenantal marriage union. Then and only then should love be fully, physically expressed between them.

Never rush love. Never awaken love before its time. Keep marital love within its God-given marital boundaries. Far from being a sensual or seductive book, the Song of Solomon three times pleads young people to live a life of purity and abstinence until marriage.

The Little Foxes

The second chapter contains a concise yet profound sermon on the importance of forgiveness. The king calls out to his beloved,

> "Catch for us the foxes,
> the little foxes
> that ruin the vineyards,
> our vineyards that are in bloom."
> (Song of Solomon 2:15)

What are these "little foxes"? Solomon, in his wisdom, says that he is deeply concerned about the threats to a marriage that often go unnoticed. He is speaking of the little secrets, the deceptions, the unspoken resentments, the careless and hurtful remarks, the big arguments over minor matters that can accumulate and damage a marriage. They are like little foxes that sneak into the vineyard through broken fences to steal and destroy the harvest while it is in bloom.

There is only one way to keep these "little foxes" of sin, negligence, and hurtfulness from ruining the "vineyard" of a marriage:

forgiveness. A marriage only works the way God designed it to work if both sides are continually forgiving each other.

We all have bad habits, sinful habits, and even little annoying habits. Sometimes, instead of asking forgiveness and trying to repent of those habits, we defend them. We say, "This is who I am. You took me for better or worse, so accept the fact that I'm worse than you took me for." But those habits are the very "little foxes" Solomon is warning against. Stop them dead in their tracks. When your beloved sins against you, be quick to forgive. And when you sin against your beloved, be quick to repent and ask forgiveness.

When we look at the Song of Solomon through the lens of the New Testament, the allegorical dimension of this book comes into sharp focus. King Solomon, the son of David, whom the Shulamite meets in the guise of a shepherd, represents King Jesus, the Son of David—our Good Shepherd. When we were poor and miserable, lost in sin, the Shepherd-King found us and loved us. Now we live in a rapturous love-relationship with Him—and the King and His Bride, the Church, will live happily ever after!

After reading the Song of Solomon, we will have a deeper understanding of the Great Commandment: "Love the Lord your God with all your heart and with all your soul and with all your mind" (Matthew 22:37). In this much-neglected book of the Old Testament, we find a picture of the joy that comes from loving God with a complete heart-soul-mind kind of love.

The covenant relationship of marriage so joyfully described in the Song of Solomon is an allegorical representation of the New Covenant between God and His people. As Song of Solomon 6:3

tells us, "I am my lover's and my lover is mine." What a beautiful restatement of this New Covenant truth: We belong to God and our God belongs to us.

PART IV

The Fall of the Kingdom of Israel

The nation of Israel began with God's promise to Abraham in Genesis 12:2: "I will make of you a great nation." In time, the Israelite people rose in prominence on the world stage. They escaped from slavery under Moses, conquered the Promised Land under Joshua, established a monarchy under Saul, and became a powerful empire under David and Solomon. But their kingdom began to decline before the end of Solomon's reign, when his wisdom failed and he led the nation into idolatry.

10

The Fall of Israel:
Broken Covenant, Broken Kingdom

A s a White House official, Charles Colson found Christ after
being sentenced to prison for his role in the Watergate scandal.
In 1976, he founded Prison Fellowship, an international Christian
outreach to prisoners and their families.

In the late 1990s, Colson received a phone call from Jack
Eckerd, owner of the Eckerd drugstore chain, inviting him to
Florida to learn about that state's criminal justice crisis. Colson
traveled with Eckerd, visiting prisons and speaking with officials
and advocacy groups.

When they addressed audiences, the drugstore mogul would
always introduce Colson by saying, "This is Chuck Colson, my
friend. He's born again, I'm not. I wish I were." Afterward, Colson
would talk to Eckerd about Jesus, but he would not receive Christ.
This happened many times.

Before Colson left Florida, he gave Eckard a copy of C. S. Lewis's *Mere Christianity*—the book that had drawn him to Christ. In the months that followed, they kept in touch. Finally, Eckerd told Colson he believed that Jesus had died and risen again.

Colson asked if Eckerd had confessed to God that he was a sinner, and asked Jesus to take control of his life. Yes, Eckerd said, he had. To which Colson responded, "Then you're born again!"

"No, I'm not," Eckerd said. "I haven't felt anything."

"Yes, you are," Colson said. "Pray with me right now." They prayed together over the phone—and at that time, Eckerd realized he was truly born again.

Soon afterward, Eckerd discovered that his drugstore chain sold pornographic magazines and ordered them removed from all his stores. When his staff told him that would cost the company $3 million in annual profits, he repeated, "Take them out!"

Colson later asked Eckerd if his newfound faith in Christ had prompted that decision.

"Why else would I give away three million dollars?" Eckerd said. "The Lord wouldn't let me off the hook."

Eckerd lobbied other companies to follow his lead, and many did—all because God wouldn't let Jack Eckerd off the hook.[1]

In ancient times, too, God did not let His people off the hook. He set forth His commandments and expected His people to keep them.

The Story of God's People and God's Law

The Pentateuch, the first five books of the Bible (also known as the Books of Moses or the Torah) tell the story of God creating the heavens and the earth, the fall of the human race, and the origin of the Hebrew (or Israelite) people. It tells of the exile and enslavement of the Hebrew people in Egypt, their liberation under Moses, the giving of the Law at Mount Sinai, and the death of Moses. In addition to the historical narrative, the Pentateuch gives us a code of laws, including the Ten Commandments, the rules for worship and sacrifices, and the rules for celebrating the Passover.

The history of ancient Israel continues in the books of Joshua, Judges, 1 and 2 Samuel, 1 and 2 Kings, and 1 and 2 Chronicles. These books show how respect for God's Law brings blessing to the nation—and how neglect of it leads to destruction.

At the beginning of Joshua, God commands the Israelites to conquer the land that He promised them. At the end, Joshua warns the Israelites to faithfully follow God's Law, adding,

> "Choose for yourselves this day whom you will serve, whether the gods your ancestors served beyond the Euphrates, or the gods of the Amorites, in whose land you are living. But as for me and my household, we will serve the LORD." (Joshua 24:15)

The book of Judges covers the period between Joshua's conquest of Canaan and the establishment of the kingdom of Israel in 1 and 2 Samuel. The judges served as informal national leaders during various times of crisis before there was a king. The events in Judges follow a pattern that never varies: First, the people slide into idolatry and rebellion against God. Then God disciplines them by handing them over to their pagan enemies. Third, the people cry out to God in repentance, pleading for His mercy. Fourth, God sends the people a leader—a judge—to deliver the Israelites. Fifth, the cycle repeats.

Immediately after Judges, we find a little four-chapter love story, the book of Ruth, that takes place during the same time. It tells of a Moabite woman named Ruth, a non-Jewish woman who embraces the God of Israel. After the death of her Israelite husband, Ruth tells her mother-in-law, Naomi, "Where you go I will go, and where you stay I will stay. Your people will be my people and your God my God."

So Ruth accompanied Naomi to Bethlehem. There, in the harvest fields outside the town, she met Boaz, Naomi's kinsman, and told him, "I am your servant Ruth. Spread the corner of your garment over me, since you are a guardian-redeemer of our family" (Ruth 3:9). Boaz says there is another member of the family whose claim to marrying Ruth outweighs his, but he settles the matter.

The prophetic symbolism is unmistakable—and serves as further proof of the unity of God's Word. Ruth symbolizes all the Gentiles who will join Jewish believers in worshiping Israel's Messiah. The unnamed man (possibly Boaz's elder brother) who has a legal claim on Ruth's hand in marriage represents the Law that is helpless to save mankind. Boaz, who pays the price to redeem Ruth, is a symbol of Jesus Christ, our Kinsman-Redeemer.

Boaz and Ruth married and had a son named Obed. Obed became the father of Jesse, who became the father of David, the future king of Israel—and an ancestor of Jesus the Messiah.

The Rise and Fall of Israel's Monarchy

The book of 1 Samuel begins with Samuel's birth and God's call upon his life. It tells the story of Samuel's anointing of King Saul during a time of tension and terrorism from the Philistines. When Saul proved to be disobedient, God's favor rested on David, who had led Israel to victory over its enemies. David also purchased the site where his son Solomon would later build the first Temple.

In 2 Samuel, God gives King David a promise through the prophet Nathan—a foretaste of the future reign of Jesus, the King of Kings and Lord of Lords:

> "When your days are over and you rest with your ancestors, I will raise up your offspring to succeed you, your own flesh and blood, and I will establish his kingdom. He is the one who will build a house for My Name, and I will establish the throne of his kingdom forever."
> (2 Samuel 7:12–13)

The main themes of 1 and 2 Samuel are the sovereignty of God and the concept of kingship.

The Israelites under King David were imbued with a sense of destiny and an unshakable confidence in God. They mistakenly thought that the kingdom of David was the Kingdom of God, invincible and eternal. Even when Israel began to fall away from worship of the one true God, they still believed that Israel would endure forever (much as people today smugly assume our civilization could never fall).

The books of 1 and 2 Kings record the exciting—and heartbreaking—saga of the kings of Israel. The first book opens with the scene of a very old and infirm King David, and a power struggle between two of his sons, Solomon and his half-brother Adonijah. David arranged for Solomon to be anointed king of Israel and instructed him in how to rule wisely and compassionately.

After David's death, Solomon proceeded to build the Great Temple in Jerusalem and led the nation to even greater heights of prosperity and power. Tragically, Solomon failed the test of leadership in his later years. In 1 Kings 11, we read:

> King Solomon, however, loved many foreign women besides Pharaoh's daughter—Moabites, Ammonites, Edomites, Sidonians, and Hittites. They were from nations about which the LORD had told the Israelites, "You must not intermarry with them, because they will surely turn your hearts after their gods." Nevertheless, Solomon held fast to them in love. He had seven hundred wives of royal birth and three hundred concubines, and his wives led him astray. As Solomon grew old, his wives turned his heart after other gods, and his heart was not fully devoted to the LORD his God, as the heart of David his father had been. He followed Ashtoreth the goddess of the Sidonians, and Molek the detestable god of the Ammonites. So Solomon did evil in the eyes of the Lord; he did not follow the LORD completely, as David his father had done. (1 Kings 11:1–6)

The decline of Israel began even before the end of Solomon's reign. Israel faced a clear choice: either serve Yahweh, the one true Creator-God—or the demon gods of the pagan cultures. The people made a tragic choice and began to embrace Baalism, which represented idolatry at its worst.

After Solomon's death, his son Rehoboam succeeded him as king. One of Solomon's officials, Jeroboam, led a rebellion, leading the ten northern tribes to form an independent kingdom of Israel, leaving Rehoboam with control only of the kingdom of Judah in the south.

Rehoboam was an arrogant and selfish man who oppressed the people and led the nation into immorality and idolatry. Because of Rehoboam's dismal leadership, Egypt invaded Judah and Rehoboam handed over the treasures of the Temple as tribute, turning his nation into a humiliated vassal state.

Elijah, Jezebel, and the Prophets of Baal

One of the key incidents recorded in 1 Kings is the story of King Ahab, his wife Jezebel, and the prophet Elijah. Ahab was the seventh king of Israel; Jezebel was a Phoenician princess, the daughter of King Ithobaal I of Tyre, and she instituted the worship of Baal throughout Israel. Baalism was infamous for its human sacrifices, including children. Jezebel also murdered many of the prophets of God and forced many others into hiding.

Jezebel persecuted anyone who did not bow to Baal, but a faithful remnant defied her. One of those who took a courageous stand was the prophet Elijah, who declared a holy war against King Ahab and Queen Jezebel.

Elijah challenged Jezebel's mystics—the 450 prophets of Baal—to a contest on Mount Carmel to determine whether Baal or the God of Israel was the one true God. Elijah would prepare one bull for sacrifice on the altar of God; the prophets of Baal would prepare another bull for the altar of Baal. "You call on the name of your god," Elijah said, "and I will call on the name of the LORD. The god who answers by fire—he is God."

Baal's prophets danced, shouted, and cut themselves all day long—and no fire came. Elijah taunted them, saying, "Shout louder!...Maybe [Baal] is sleeping!" When the priests had exhausted themselves, Elijah placed his sacrifice on the wood of the altar and had it all doused with water three times.

Then, with calm dignity, he prayed,

> "LORD, the God of Abraham, Isaac, and Israel, let it be known today that You are God in Israel and that I am your servant and have done all these things at your command. Answer me, LORD, answer me, so these people will know that You, LORD, are God, and that You are turning their hearts back again." (1 Kings 18:36–37)

Immediately, fire fell from Heaven, consumed the sacrificial bull, the wood, the water, and even the stones of the altar. All the people who witnessed this miracle cried out, "The LORD—He is God!"

Then Elijah ordered the people to seize and kill the prophets of Baal and Asherah. Later, God decreed the death of Queen Jezebel and King Ahab and the annihilation of Ahab's royal line.

Though Israel was cleansed of these two corrupt political figures, neither the kingdom of Israel nor the kingdom of Judah was the Kingdom of God. No political state, led by mere human beings, could ever be God's eternal Kingdom.

Exile and Captivity

The rest of the narrative of 1 and 2 Kings—written during the Babylonian exile, approximately 550 to 560 BC—tells a story of a line of kings in both Israel and Judah. Some of the kings were good, some were evil. God judged each according to whether he kept the Law. Again and again, the kings of both Israel and Judah failed the test and led their people into idolatry. And the nation paid the price.

The books of 1 and 2 Chronicles cover much of the same history as 1 and 2 Kings—but from a different perspective and for a different purpose. The books of Chronicles were written around 450 to 440 BC, after the exile had ended, and have a more encouraging tone, meant to increase the faith of Jews who were rebuilding their lives after the captivity.

The books of Kings warned that the troubles of Israel and Judah were not the result of God's abandonment, but of the people's disobedience. The books of Chronicles devote more space to the nation's triumphs than its failures and encouraged the nation to seek revival and restoration.

Ezra tells how the Jews returned to Judah after seventy years of exile in Babylon. The book of Nehemiah continues the story, focusing on the rebuilding of Jerusalem in times of stress and adversity.

The book of Esther tells the gripping story of a Jewish girl in Persia (her birth name was Hadassah, but she became known as Esther). Through her courage and willingness to sacrifice herself, she became queen of Persia during the reign of King Ahasuerus from 486 to 465 BC and saved her people from genocide. Though the book does not directly mention God by name, His hand can be seen moving events throughout the story.

These books of ancient Jewish history are followed by the books of the prophets.

From Godliness to Godlessness

The prophetic books consist of the last seventeen books of the Old Testament. They are divided between the five "major prophets" (Isaiah, Jeremiah, Lamentations, Ezekiel, Daniel) and the twelve "minor prophets" (Hosea, Joel, Amos, Obadiah, Jonah, Micah, Nahum, Habakkuk, Zephaniah, Haggai, Zechariah, and Malachi). The terms "major" and "minor" refer to the length of the books, not their importance. Every book of the Bible is vitally important to us and to God, regardless of length.

The prophetic books show us the tremendous importance of God's Law and what it meant under the Old Covenant. Again and again, throughout Israel's history, the prophets denounced the nation's sin, idolatry, and injustice. They would not let God's people "off the hook," repeatedly calling them to repentance.

The Old Covenant can be fulfilled only by faith in Christ—not by works, not by keeping the Law. As Paul tells us in his letter to the Romans,

> Therefore no one will be declared righteous in God's sight by the works of the Law; rather, through the Law we become conscious of our sin. But now apart from the Law the righteousness of God has been made known, to which the Law and the Prophets testify. This righteousness is given through faith in Jesus Christ to all who believe. (Romans 3:20–22)

And as he told the Christians in Galatia,

> A person is not justified by the works of the Law, but by faith in Jesus Christ. So we, too, have put our faith in Christ Jesus that we may be justified by faith in Christ and not by the works of the Law, because by the works of the Law no one will be justified. (Galatians 2:16)

The prophetic books chronicle the decline and fall of Israel and Judah because they neglected God's Law, rejected the Old Covenant, and descended into wickedness and idolatry.

This was no gentle slide into compromise. Human beings take on the character of the gods they serve—and Baal was as evil and depraved as a pagan deity could be. There is no comparing Yahweh to Baal. The God of Israel had called Israel to a life of obedience and faith. He had entered into a covenant with them and promised them a glorious destiny as His beloved people. Baal, by contrast, represented the very antithesis of covenant-keeping. Like Astarte, Asherah, Anat, and the other demonic deities of the surrounding tribes, he was unpredictable, untrustworthy, and represented forces and functions connected with storms, seasons, and fertility. The Baal cult was closely linked to death and rebirth. The false prophets of Baal used rituals and sacrifices—including horrifying human sacrifices—in an attempt to control nature and increase fruitfulness in crops, herds, and human populations.

The worship of Baal was completely opposed to the pure worship of Yahweh. As God said through the prophet Jeremiah:

> For they have forsaken Me and made this a place of foreign gods; they have burned incense in it to gods that neither they nor their ancestors nor the kings of Judah ever knew, and they have filled this place with the blood of the innocent. They have built the high places of Baal to burn their children in the fire as offerings to Baal—something I did not command or mention, nor did it enter My mind. (Jeremiah 19:4–5)

As Baalism exerted its corrosive influence in Israelite society, even those who did not sacrifice to Baal began referring to Yahweh by the blasphemous name of Baal.

Into this world of corruption and moral chaos, the prophets emerged.

11

The Major Prophets: Thunder in the Kingdom

Someone once said, "An historian is a reversed prophet." It's true. An historian looks back on major events in the past. Prophets warn against—and sometimes predict—major events in the future. Most biblical prophecies were warnings that tragically went unheeded by Israel and Judah.

But an astonishing number of Old Testament predictions have already been fulfilled with stunning accuracy and precision. Many of those are found in the books of the "major prophets": Isaiah, Jeremiah, Lamentations, Ezekiel, and Daniel.

God has never broken His word. Because so many of His promises have already been fulfilled, we have an objective reason to believe Him. Let's look at the warnings and promises in the prophetic books of the Old Testament.

Isaiah: Prophet of the Servant and the King

Isaiah is one of the most compelling books in the Bible. The first chapter records God's promise to forgive and give us a new beginning:

> "Come now, let us settle the matter,"
> says the LORD.
> "Though your sins are like scarlet,
> they shall be as white as snow;
> though they are red as crimson,
> they shall be like wool." (Isaiah 1:18)

This is where we first hear of a remnant of God's people being spared amid the destruction of the Jewish nation. Isaiah also shows us that the Kingdom of God should not be confused with any earthly kingdom. It says several times that the Messiah would be born of King David's lineage, and that He would establish an *eternal* Kingdom. For example:

> For to us a child is born,
> to us a son is given,
> and the government will be on His shoulders.
> And He will be called
> Wonderful Counselor, Mighty God,
> Everlasting Father, Prince of Peace.
> Of the greatness of His government and peace
> there will be no end.
> He will reign on David's throne
> and over his kingdom,
> establishing and upholding it

with justice and righteousness
from that time on and forever. (Isaiah 9:6–7)

God also promised, "A shoot will come up from the stump of Jesse; from his roots a Branch will bear fruit. The Spirit of the LORD will rest on him" (Isaiah 11:1–2). Jesse is David's father. "The stump of Jesse" tells us that their lineage would be cut off. This took place when the Assyrians cut off the monarchy of the northern kingdom of Israel and the Babylonians cut off the monarchy of Judah. Yet some descendants of David remained, and from one of them—a virgin named Mary—a child was born: a "shoot" from the "stump of Jesse."

Isaiah also promises that a Suffering Servant would come. He would be despised, rejected, and pierced for our sins:

He grew up before him like a tender shoot,
and like a root out of dry ground.
He had no beauty or majesty to attract us to Him,
nothing in His appearance that we should desire Him.
He was despised and rejected by mankind,
a man of suffering, and familiar with pain.
Like one from whom people hide their faces
He was despised, and we held Him in low esteem.
Surely He took up our pain
and bore our suffering,
yet we considered Him punished by God,
stricken by Him, and afflicted.
But He was pierced for our transgressions,
He was crushed for our iniquities;
the punishment that brought us peace was on Him,

and by His wounds we are healed.
We all, like sheep, have gone astray,
each of us has turned to our own way;
and the LORD has laid on Him
the iniquity of us all. (Isaiah 53:2–6)

This is Isaiah's prophetic vision of the pierced and crucified Messiah upon the cross. This is God's promise of His atoning grace, laying our sin upon the Suffering Servant, so that we might be healed by His wounds.

Jesus the Messiah, the Prince of the line of David, will one day rule over a faithful remnant, the redeemed Israel. The history of the entire world is moving toward the establishment of the Kingdom of God. But the Messiah could not come to a proud nation at the height of its political glory. He could only come to a severed stump of a nation.

The Jewish people didn't understand the true nature of the coming Kingdom or its King. They were thinking in political terms. As a result, every new king in Israel or Judah was, in their minds, potentially the Messiah. This illusion persisted even after the resurrection of Jesus, when His followers asked Him, "Lord, are you at this time going to restore the kingdom to Israel?" (Acts 1:6). They didn't understand (but would soon learn) that the hope of God's people had shifted from the nation of Israel to the church of Jesus Christ.

All the prophets from Isaiah to Malachi recognized that a new spiritual Israel (not the political nation) would inherit the promised Kingdom of God. The New Testament church saw itself as this new spiritual "Israel."

Isaiah tells us that God intends to rule over the entire earth, not merely a plot of real estate in Palestine. The true God of Israel does not belong to any one race, culture, or nation. He is the God of all who obey Him, anywhere on Earth:

> "Turn to Me and be saved,
> all you ends of the earth;
> for I am God, and there is no other.
> By Myself I have sworn,
> My mouth has uttered in all integrity
> a word that will not be revoked:
> Before Me every knee will bow;
> by Me every tongue will swear." (Isaiah 45:22–23)

God controls history. At the end, He will establish His reign over all the earth. The words of God, spoken through Isaiah, anticipate the words of Jesus:

> "I say to you that many will come from the east and the west, and will take their places at the feast with Abraham, Isaac, and Jacob in the kingdom of heaven." (Matthew 8:11)

Isaiah reminds us that a moral, just, and peaceful world order is impossible without submission to the righteous rule of God. Through Isaiah, God promises that this world order will arrive one day:

> They will neither harm nor destroy
> on all My holy mountain,
> for the earth will be filled
> with the knowledge of the LORD
> as the waters cover the sea. (Isaiah 11:9)

The human race will never know peace apart from the Kingdom of God. Lasting peace cannot be achieved by politics or scientific progress or even organized religion. True peace will come only when all people submit to the rule of the true King. It will come as an answer to the prayer Jesus taught us to pray, "Our Father in heaven, hallowed be your name, your kingdom come, your will be done, on earth as it is in heaven" (Matthew 6:9–10).

Jeremiah: The Prophet Who Confronted Kings

Jeremiah is a book of warnings and laments. Jeremiah was called by God as a prophet in the thirteenth year of Josiah, king of Judah, in 626 BC. He served as a prophet for nearly forty years, during the reign of five kings of Judah. Again and again, he warned of God's judgment against Judah—until his warnings finally came to pass with the fall of Jerusalem and the destruction of Solomon's Temple in 587 BC.

Israel had reached a state of extreme corruption and idolatry. The people worshiped idols and burned their own children as sacrifices on the altars of Baal. Jeremiah warned the people that God would not allow their idolatry to go unpunished. But the wicked kings, greedy priests, and false prophets would not listen.

So God had no choice but to withdraw His blessings from Judah. As a result, the Babylonian army starved and conquered Jerusalem, and the people were led away into captivity.

Here again, we see that Judah was not the Kingdom of God. Why? Because Judah had broken the Covenant. God shifted His focus entirely from the Jewish state to a small, faithful remnant, with whom He will one day make a New Covenant. The people of the New Covenant will be the people of God's Kingdom. They will be people with clean hands and clean hearts. God will only rule over an obedient people.

The kings of Judah in the time of Jeremiah—such as Joachim and Zedekiah—were godless, selfish, corrupt, and idolatrous. Jeremiah rejected the political state as the vehicle of God's Kingdom because it reflected the immorality and apostasy of its leaders.

Jeremiah's message arises again and again in God's Word: If we choose sin, rebellion, and false gods, then God will let us go our own way. He will allow us to suffer the consequences of our willful choices, which lead to desolation.

But while there is time remaining, there is always an opportunity to return to God and find salvation. He does not reject us, even when we abandon Him. If we turn to God with repentant hearts, He will receive us and welcome us home.

People who encounter the book of Jeremiah for the first time are often surprised by the struggles Jeremiah endured against political and religious leaders, the people, and even God. In his sorrow, Jeremiah writes:

Oh, that I had in the desert
a lodging place for travelers,
so that I might leave my people
and go away from them;
for they are all adulterers,
a crowd of unfaithful people. (Jeremiah 9:2)

Through Jeremiah, God shows us that He welcomes our most troubled emotions, even when they are directed at Him. The prophet candidly, even angrily complains to God, pouring out his complaints and his feeling that God has misled him:

I never sat in the company of revelers,
never made merry with them;
I sat alone because your hand was on me
and You had filled me with indignation.
Why is my pain unending
and my wound grievous and incurable?
You are to me like a deceptive brook,
like a spring that fails. (Jeremiah 15:17–18)

God did not condemn Jeremiah, yet He did not want the prophet to remain mired in anger and self-pity. He urged him to pull out of his emotional nosedive and focus on the future to which God had called him:

"If you repent, I will restore you
that you may serve Me;
if you utter worthy, not worthless, words,
you will be My spokesman." (Jeremiah 15:19)

Later, when Jeremiah reaches the absolute pit of his despair, he pours out his anguish to God. Again, God understands and does not rebuke him for them:

Cursed be the day I was born!
May the day my mother bore me not be blessed!
Cursed be the man who brought my father the news,
who made him very glad, saying,
"A child is born to you—a son!"
May that man be like the towns
the LORD overthrew without pity.

May he hear wailing in the morning,
a battle cry at noon.
For he did not kill me in the womb,
with my mother as my grave,
her womb enlarged forever.
Why did I ever come out of the womb
to see trouble and sorrow
and to end my days in shame?
(Jeremiah 20:14–18)

We wince at these bitter words—yet we shouldn't be quick to judge Jeremiah. Who among us could have withstood the pressures, threats, and disappointments that he endured?

Jeremiah had an intense personality and a strong sense of duty. You would not consider him a calm and even-tempered man. He wrestled with men and with God. He boldly confronted kings. He was often persecuted and threatened with death.

After he warned King Zedekiah that Jerusalem would fall to the Babylonians, the king's officials demanded Jeremiah be killed. Zedekiah gave the prophet's enemies permission to seize him. The conspirators placed Jeremiah at the bottom of a deep cistern, leaving him to starve to death. He was rescued by an Ethiopian, but his enemies later accused him of aiding the Babylonians and threw him in prison (see Jeremiah 37).

Jeremiah suffered deeply because he loved these wayward people of Judah. His pain was "unending" and his emotional wound was "grievous and incurable" because he wanted to save them from their foolishness and sin. But they wouldn't listen.

Jeremiah's grief reminds us of the sorrow of Jesus Himself, who mourned,

"Jerusalem, Jerusalem, you who kill the prophets and stone those sent to you, how often I have longed to gather your children together, as a hen gathers her chicks under her wings, and you were not willing." (Matthew 23:37)

After the Babylonians conquered Jerusalem, the commander of the Babylonian imperial guard released Jeremiah from his chains, saying,

"The LORD your God decreed this disaster for this place. And now the LORD has brought it about; He has done just as He said He would. All this happened because you people sinned against the LORD and did not obey Him. But today I am freeing you from the chains on your wrists." (Jeremiah 40:2–4)

This Babylonian soldier had more respect for the God of Israel than the people of Jerusalem did. He understood that the Babylonians' victory was due to the Jews' sin and idolatry.

After most of the people of Jerusalem were taken into captivity in Babylon, God moved King Nebuchadnezzar to carry out His will.

It's important to understand that a major shift of focus takes place in the biblical narrative at this point in Jeremiah 40. From Genesis, when God promised to make of Abraham a great nation, right up to the destruction of Jerusalem, the Bible focuses on the political kingdoms of Israel and Judah. Now both Israel and Judah have been conquered. Jerusalem is destroyed. And the biblical narrative focuses not on the political nation, but on a tiny remnant in Judah.

This remnant is a tiny vestige of people with whom God will one day make a New Covenant. And here we see a crucial biblical principle at work: *Only those who have seen the total failure of the earthly order will ultimately hope for the Kingdom of God.*

This is not to say that, after God's original plan for Israel failed, He switched to Plan B. It was *never* God's plan for the political kingdom of Israel or Judah to become the Kingdom of God.

The writer of Hebrews said that when Abraham left his home in Ur and journeyed to the Promised Land, "he was looking forward to the city with foundations, whose architect and builder is God" (Hebrews 11:10). Similarly, the Apostle Paul describes the city Abraham looked forward to as "a building from God, an eternal house in heaven, not built by human hands" (2 Corinthians 5:1). That is the true Kingdom of God.

Jeremiah's message to his people—and to us—is that you don't need sacrifices, rituals, or a Temple in order to worship God. True worship is not an outward ritual, but an obedient heart:

> This is what the LORD Almighty, the God of Israel, says: "Go ahead, add your burnt offerings to your other sacrifices and eat the meat yourselves! For when I brought your ancestors out of Egypt and spoke to them, I did not just give them commands about burnt offerings and sacrifices, but I gave them this command: Obey Me, and I will be your God and you will be My people. Walk in obedience to all I command you, that it may go well with you." (Jeremiah 7:21–23)

Those who call upon God in obedient faith will find that He is leading them toward a future of blessing and belonging:

"For I know the plans I have for you," declares the LORD, "plans to prosper you and not to harm you, plans to give you hope and a future. Then you will call on Me and come and pray to Me, and I will listen to you. You will seek Me and find Me when you seek Me with all your heart. I will be found by you," declares the Lord, "and will bring you back from captivity. I will gather you from all the nations and places where I have banished you," declares the Lord, "and will bring you back to the place from which I carried you into exile." (Jeremiah 29:11–14)

Jeremiah also proclaims the coming of a New Covenant with a New Israel:

"The days are coming," declares the LORD,
"when I will make a new covenant
with the people of Israel
and with the people of Judah....
I will put My law in their minds
and write it on their hearts.
I will be their God,
and they will be My people.
No longer will they teach their neighbor,
or say to one another, 'Know the LORD,'
because they will all know me,
from the least of them to the greatest,"
declares the LORD.
"For I will forgive their wickedness
 and will remember their sins no more."
(Jeremiah 31:31, 33–34)

The Jewish people longed only for the restoration of the Jewish nation. But Jeremiah envisioned a transcendent hope for a new Kingdom, under a New Covenant, empowered by the Spirit of God. The next time we find similar words in the Bible is in Matthew 26:28, where Jesus, at the Last Supper, tells the disciples, "This is My blood of the covenant, which is poured out for many for the forgiveness of sins."

Lamentations: Out of Desolation, Hope!

Jeremiah also wrote the book of Lamentations. It reflects the prophet's sorrow over the destruction of Jerusalem and the Jews' exile to Babylon. The book is so intense in its emotions that, at times, it reads like an indictment against God for allowing the destruction of Judah. Yet Jeremiah had spent decades warning the people that their idolatries and abominations would lead to this very end. "I am the man who has seen affliction by the rod of the LORD's wrath," he laments. "He has driven me away and made me walk in darkness rather than light" (Lamentations 3:1–2).

But Jeremiah ultimately comes to a place of peace with and hope in God. In the same chapter, he writes these words of comfort and faith:

> Yet this I call to mind
> and therefore I have hope:
> Because of the LORD's great love we are not consumed,
> for His compassions never fail.
> They are new every morning;
> great is your faithfulness.
> I say to myself, "The LORD is my portion;

therefore I will wait for Him."
The LORD is good to those whose hope is in Him,
to the one who seeks Him;
it is good to wait quietly
for the salvation of the LORD. (Lamentations 3:21–26)

Out of the desolate ruins of Jerusalem, a word of hope emerges. Each chapter of Lamentations discloses a personal message from God for our times of sorrow, loss, and desolation. He never abandons us. His compassion never fails. This book is good medicine for times of sorrow.

Ezekiel: A Promise of Restoration

Ezekiel focuses on prophecies of destruction and the promised restoration of the land of Israel. The name "Ezekiel" means "God is strong," and the strength and power of God are on full display in this compelling book, which records six intense visions that God gave the prophets during his exile in Babylon. These are divided into three main themes:

1. God's judgment against Israel (Ezekiel 1–24). Ezekiel 1 describes the Throne Vision, in which Ezekiel saw fire, lightning, sparkling wheels rimmed with eyes, angelic beings, and a great throne with a glorious, glowing, man-like figure: "the appearance of the likeness of the glory of the Lord." In the First Temple Vision (Ezekiel 8), the prophet sees God depart from the Temple because false idols are being worshiped there. The Images of Israel section (Ezekiel 15–19) depicts the nation of Israel as fuel for a fire, an abandoned child rescued by God, a brazen prostitute engaged in detestable acts, and more.

2. God's judgment against enemy nations (Ezekiel 25–32).

3. God's future blessings for Israel: a new beginning and a new Temple (Ezekiel 33–48). The Vision of the Dry Bones (Ezekiel 37) depicts Israel as a valley of dry bones which, upon God's command, come to life and become a vast army—an image of hope for Israel's future.

The Vision of Gog and Magog (Ezekiel 38 and 39) promises a day of judgment for Israel's enemies, followed by an age of peace in which God pledges, "I will pour out My Spirit on the people of Israel."

The Final Temple Vision (Ezekiel 40–48) describes a future Temple in a new Jerusalem.

Ezekiel was written after the kingdom of Judah had fallen, never again to rise. While some people doubted that God was in control, others grumbled that He was unfair.

This period marks the beginning of the Diaspora, the great dispersion and oppression of the Jewish people. The Jews in Palestine who escaped death or deportation looked for better opportunities elsewhere. The Bible records the beginning of this tremendous migration, first to Egypt (see Jeremiah 43 and 44 and Isaiah 19:18) and eventually throughout the known world. Palestine, however, continued to be the spiritual homeland of the Jews, and they longed for a revived nation there.

The Babylonian exile was a calamity for the Jewish people and the Jewish religion. The most popular false prophets in Israel and Judah had promised that God would never allow His nation to fall, yet the unthinkable had come to pass. God had delivered the Jewish kingdom into the hands of foreign enemies who worshiped pagan gods.

This forced many Jews to reconsider their faith in God. Was the Jewish religion merely the parochial creed of one failed nation in

Palestine? Or was faith in Yahweh deep enough to be transplanted into every nation of the world? Paradoxically, the Babylonian exile, far from being the graveyard of Israel's faith in God, proved to be a time of great spiritual renewal and vitality. As God told Ezekiel, "But I will spare some, for some of you will escape the sword when you are scattered among the lands and nations" (Ezekiel 6:8). There also would be a future revival:

> "For I will take you out of the nations; I will gather you
> from all the countries and bring you back into your own
> land. I will sprinkle clean water on you, and you will be
> clean; I will cleanse you from all your impurities and
> from all your idols. I will give you a new heart and put
> a new spirit in you; I will remove from you your heart
> of stone and give you a heart of flesh. And I will put My
> Spirit in you and move you to follow My decrees and be
> careful to keep My laws. Then you will live in the land
> I gave your ancestors; you will be My people, and I will
> be your God." (Ezekiel 36:24–28)

The book concludes, "And the name of the city from that time on will be: THE LORD IS THERE" (Ezekiel 48:35). This is Ezekiel's vision of the coming Kingdom of God.

Daniel: Powerful Stories, a Remarkable Timetable

The book of Daniel recounts the life and visions of the prophet Daniel, who lived in exile in Babylon. The book combines history and prophecy, including of the coming Messiah and the End Time.

The theme is that, just as God miraculously rescued Daniel from a den of lions, He also would rescue Israel.

The book has two parts. Part 1 (chapters 1–6) contains six narratives:

1. Daniel and his friends maintain their purity and principles in the court of King Nebuchadnezzar (chapter 1).
2. Nebuchadnezzar's dream of four kingdoms (chapter 2).
3. The fiery furnace (chapter 3).
4. Nebuchadnezzar's ordeal of insanity (chapter 4).
5. The handwriting on the wall and the fall of Babylon (chapter 5).
6. Daniel in the lions' den (chapter 6).

Part 2 contains four prophetic visions which include messianic prophecies that shed additional light on the messianic prophecies in Isaiah and elsewhere.

In Daniel 7, we find a prophecy that the Messiah (whom Daniel calls the "Ancient of Days") will have an everlasting Kingdom. In his vision, Daniel saw that the Messiah was given authority, glory, and sovereign power; all nations and peoples of every language worshiped Him. His dominion is an everlasting dominion that will not pass away, and His Kingdom is one that will never be destroyed. (Daniel 7:13–14)

And in Daniel 9, the prophet relates a vision that predicts the exact time of the arrival of Jesus the Messiah, His death, and the

destruction of Jerusalem and the Temple of Herod by Rome in
AD 70:

> "Know and understand this: From the time the word
> goes out to restore and rebuild Jerusalem until the
> Anointed One, the ruler, comes, there will be seven
> 'sevens,' and sixty-two 'sevens.' It will be rebuilt with
> streets and a trench, but in times of trouble. After the
> sixty-two 'sevens,' the Anointed One will be put to death
> and will have nothing. The people of the ruler who will
> come will destroy the city and the sanctuary. The end
> will come like a flood: War will continue until the end,
> and desolations have been decreed." (Daniel 9:25–26)

Since the nineteenth century, Bible scholars have calculated the
meaning of the "seven 'sevens,' and sixty-two 'sevens'" and realized
that it worked out to a precise prediction of the arrival of Jesus in
Jerusalem on Palm Sunday, when He was heralded as Israel's king.
In his book *The Coming Prince*, Sir Robert Anderson determined
that Daniel predicted a period of 483 years from the decree of the
Persian king Artaxerxes to rebuild Jerusalem until the Lord's arrival
in Jerusalem on a donkey. The other astonishing predictions in
these verses are that "the Anointed One will be put to death" and
the "people of the ruler who will come will destroy the city and the
sanctuary," all of which have been fulfilled.

The book of Daniel also sets an excellent example for young
Christians because it tells the story of young people taking a courageous, uncompromised stand for God in a godless and hostile
world.

God has not changed. He still rescues His people from the "lions' den" of our godless culture today.

12

"Minor" Prophets, Major Impact

I recently heard about a Christmas Eve gathering of Christian friends. As they were talking, the conversation turned to thoughts of Heaven.

One mature believer said, "I wonder what language we'll speak in Heaven."

Another mature believer said, "Maybe we'll all speak in our own language, but we'll understand all the other languages."

Yet another said, "Maybe we'll speak a spiritual language, unique to Heaven."

These older friends traded opinions and speculations until one young man, a college student, cleared his throat and said, "I know the answer."

All eyes turned to him. "You do?" someone said. "How do you know?"

"I read it in my morning devotions," the young man said. "It's in Zephaniah 3:9 in the English Standard Version: 'For at that time I will change the speech of the peoples to a pure speech, that all of them may call upon the name of the Lord and serve Him with one accord.'"

All the mature believers in that room took a lesson from the young college student in their midst: If you want answers to your questions about God and eternity, you probably don't need to speculate. You simply need to read the answer God has already given in His Word.[1]

In this case, the answer to a fascinating question about Heaven came from Zephaniah, one of the so-called "minor prophets" of the Old Testament. But as we're about to see, the impact of the "minor prophets" on our understanding of God's prophetic agenda is anything but minor.

Hosea: A Tale of Redemptive Love

The book of Hosea tells the story of a beautiful romance, heartbreaking unfaithfulness, and redemptive love. It is set during the decline of the northern kingdom of Israel, shortly before it was conquered by Assyria.

God told the prophet Hosea, "Go, marry a promiscuous woman and have children with her, for like an adulterous wife this land is guilty of unfaithfulness to the Lord." So Hosea obediently married a prostitute named Gomer, and she bore him a son.

Hosea's faithless wife led the prophet through heartbreaking humiliation. But Hosea—who symbolizes God in His relationship to faithless Israel—was full of forgiving love for Gomer. Finally, his unfailing love won her back and their relationship was restored.

This allegory teaches us volumes about the love of God. Even though we reject Him and rebel against Him, even though we have broken His heart, He stands ready to redeem us and restore us. He is a God of relentless love.

Joel: A Prophecy of Devastation—and Renewal

The book of Joel shows how God is involved in shaping the history of Israel and the surrounding nations. This brief book opens with a description of a devastating locust swarm. There probably was an actual locust swarm that devastated the crops of Israel, yet it is also a fitting metaphor for the destruction caused by Israel's enemies. But even though Israel lay desolate afterward, God promised a bright future after the nation repents:

> "I will repay you for the years the locusts have eaten—
> the great locust and the young locust,
> the other locusts and the locust swarm—
> My great army that I sent among you....
> Then you will know that I am in Israel,
> that I am the LORD your God,
> and that there is no other;
> never again will My people be shamed.
> And afterward,
> I will pour out My Spirit on all people.
> Your sons and daughters will prophesy,
> your old men will dream dreams,
> your young men will see visions." (Joel 2:25, 27–28)

If you feel as if your life has been devastated by "locusts," the consequences of your sin, God promises to restore you and reestablish you—if you will turn back to Him in faith and repentance.

Amos: "Let Justice Roll"

Amos is probably the earliest of the prophetic books. Amos came from the southern kingdom of Judah but he preached in the northern kingdom of Israel. The themes of the book of Amos are God's power, judgment, and demand that all people, especially the poor and powerless, be treated justly.

Amos tells Israel that God will judge His own chosen people with the same standard He judges the heathen nations. He also warns that God will reject their religious rites and sacrifices if they do not repent of their sins and acts of oppression:

> "I hate, I despise your religious festivals;
> your assemblies are a stench to Me.
> Even though you bring Me burnt offerings and grain
> offerings,
> I will not accept them.
> Though you bring choice fellowship offerings,
> I will have no regard for them.
> Away with the noise of your songs!
> I will not listen to the music of your harps.
> But let justice roll on like a river,
> righteousness like a never-failing stream!"
> (Amos 5:21–24)

The central theme of the book is that a corrupt, selfish, idolatrous society is terminally ill. Such a society is under God's judgment. If God's people fail to take a stand and speak out against it, they have ceased to have an influence—or any reason for existing. No amount of religious activity can build the Kingdom of God. Correct doctrine is no substitute for obedience to God's will. God wants to reign in our everyday lives.

Amos preached to the nation about the need to reactivate faith in—and obedience to—God's Covenant. He reminded the Jews that they were God's people and subjects of His sovereign rule. As such, they had a solemn responsibility before God.

Speaking through Amos, God warns that Israel is at risk:

> "Surely the eyes of the Sovereign LORD
> are on the sinful kingdom.
> I will destroy it
> from the face of the earth.
> Yet I will not totally destroy
> the descendants of Jacob,"
> declares the LORD. (Amos 9:8)

The kingdom of Israel, then, was not and could not be the Kingdom of God because it was under the judgment of God.

The smug and complacent people were looking forward to the "day of the Lord" because they thought it would be the day in which Israel would be confirmed as the Kingdom of God. But God, through Amos, declared that the "day of the Lord" would be a day of judgment and doom for the disobedient nation:

> Woe to you who long
> for the day of the LORD!
> Why do you long for the day of the LORD?
> That day will be darkness, not light.
> It will be as though a man fled from a lion
> only to meet a bear,
> as though he entered his house
> and rested his hand on the wall
> only to have a snake bite him.

> Will not the day of the LORD be darkness, not light—
> pitch-dark, without a ray of brightness? (Amos 5:18–20)

Amos affirmed that God would not defend the ancient state of Israel when the Assyrians came. Israel's hope in the political kingdom would be irrevocably shattered. The story of Israel's swift destruction, as Amos predicted, is found in 2 Kings 15–17.

But that did not mean all hope was lost. God promised that His people would be restored—not politically, but spiritually—when His true, eternal Kingdom was established.

Obadiah: Jacob versus Esau

Obadiah is the shortest book in the Old Testament, consisting of a single chapter. It was written around 590 BC, after the fall of both Israel and Judah. Obadiah pronounces God's judgment against the people of Edom, who are gloating over the defeat of the Jews. (The Edomites, in fact, helped the Babylonians loot the city of Jerusalem and enslave its people in 597 BC.)

Who were the Edomites? They were descendants of Esau, the brother of Jacob. Just as Jacob and Esau engaged in a fierce sibling rivalry, the Israelites and the Edomites continually clashed. Obadiah warns:

> You should not gloat over your brother
> in the day of his misfortune,
> nor rejoice over the people of Judah
> in the day of their destruction,
> nor boast so much
> in the day of their trouble.

You should not march through the gates of my people
in the day of their disaster,
nor gloat over them in their calamity
in the day of their disaster,
nor seize their wealth
in the day of their disaster. (Obadiah 1:12–13)

But the book is much more than a rebuke to Edom—it's a message of hope and ultimate victory for the Jewish people. Jacob and Esau, the Jews and the Edomites, represent two ways of life. Jacob represents obedience, Esau represents rebellion. Even though "Jacob" (the Jewish nation) has sinned and failed God, a day is coming when the repentant one will be restored. Obadiah predicts the nation's coming victory:

Jacob will be a fire
and Joseph a flame;
Esau will be stubble,
and they will set him on fire and destroy him.
There will be no survivors
from Esau....
Deliverers will go up on Mount Zion
to govern the mountains of Esau.
And the kingdom will be the Lord's. (Obadiah 1:18, 21)

Jonah: The Reluctant Prophet

The book of Jonah contains one of the most famous stories in the Bible. But even though it is only four chapters long, I wonder how many people truly understand it in detail. Jonah is filled with perceptive insight into human nature, which has not changed in all the centuries since the book was written.

When God commands Jonah to go to the Assyrian capital of Nineveh and preach against the wickedness of the people, he tries to run away. He goes to the port town of Jaffa and boards a ship bound for distant Tarshish. Mid-voyage, a fierce storm rises, threatening to sink the ship. The sailors cast lots, which point to Jonah as the cause of their peril. Jonah confesses he is the cause, and urges the sailors to throw him overboard. Reluctantly, the sailors cast Jonah into the sea—and the storm ceases to blow. As a result, the sailors are converted to faith in the God of Israel.

Meanwhile, Jonah is swallowed by a gigantic fish and spends three days and three nights in its belly, where he prays to God in his affliction. God commands the fish to vomit Jonah onto the beach. Chastened and repentant, Jonah travels to Nineveh, which was probably the largest city in the world at that time. He preached that, unless the people repented, Nineveh would be overthrown. Jonah was astonished to see that all the Ninevites, from the king on down, repented with prayer, fasting, and sackcloth and ashes.

Annoyed that God had granted grace to the repentant Ninevites, Jonah leaves the city, makes a shelter in the desert, and pouts. He tells God, "Isn't this what I said, LORD, when I was still at home? That is what I tried to forestall by fleeing to Tarshish. I knew that You are a gracious and compassionate God, slow to anger and abounding in love, a God who relents from sending calamity. Now, Lord, take away my life, for it is better for me to die than to live" (Jonah 4:2–3). Jonah would rather have died than seen the Ninevites live.

God provides a leafy plant to give shade to Jonah—and he loves it! The next day, God sends a worm to kill the plant—and Jonah is heartbroken and angry to the point of wishing himself dead. God rebukes Jonah for being heartbroken over the plant while wishing death on more than 120,000 humans in Nineveh.

The story ends with God's rebuke and confronts us with several questions: Are we running away from God's call upon our lives? Are we avoiding His command to spread His good news to our family, friends, and neighbors? Do we care as much about the lost souls around us as we care about our own comfort?

Micah: Signpost to Bethlehem

In Micah, God warns those who oppress the poor, condemns unjust leaders who take bribes, and predicts an eventual time of world peace when the Lord reigns from Zion:

In the last days
the mountain of the LORD's temple will be established
as the highest of the mountains;
it will be exalted above the hills,
and peoples will stream to it.
Many nations will come and say,
"Come, let us go up to the mountain of the LORD,
to the temple of the God of Jacob.
He will teach us His ways,
so that we may walk in His paths."
The law will go out from Zion,
the word of the LORD from Jerusalem. (Micah 4:1–2)

The book is also the source of the beloved prophecy that the Messiah will be born in Bethlehem:

"But you, Bethlehem Ephrathah,
though you are small among the clans of Judah,
out of you will come for me
one who will be ruler over Israel,
whose origins are from of old,
from ancient times." (Micah 5:2)

This book also contains these beloved words: "And what does the LORD require of you? To act justly and to love mercy and to walk humbly with your God" (Micah 6:8).

Nahum: A Prophecy of Destruction

Nahum vividly predicts the destruction of Nineveh, calling it "the city of blood, full of lies, full of plunder, never without victims" (Nahum 3:1). Apparently, the repentance of the Ninevites in Jonah's time didn't last, because Nahum was required to speak out against its wickedness again and predict its fall. Just as Nahum prophesied, the forces of Babylon and the Medes surrounded the city in 625 BC, laying siege for three months and finally burning it to the ground.

Despite the angry, vengeful tone of much of this short book, Nahum also speaks of God's unchanging love and righteousness. God demands justice and punishes ungodliness and violence against the innocent. That is why the prophet tells us,

The LORD is good,
a refuge in times of trouble.
He cares for those who trust in Him,
but with an overwhelming flood
He will make an end of Nineveh. (Nahum 1:7–8)

Habakkuk: The Just Shall Live by Faith

Habakkuk has played a profound role in Christian theology. It opens with these age-old questions:

> "How long, LORD, must I call for help,
> but You do not listen?
> Or cry out to You, 'Violence!'
> but You do not save?
> Why do You make me look at injustice?
> Why do You tolerate wrongdoing?" (Habakkuk 1:2–3)

In two of his great letters, Romans and Galatians, the Apostle Paul cites Habakkuk 2:4: "The just shall live by His faith" (KJV). This statement is also a foundational concept in Hebrews and helped spark the Protestant Reformation by igniting a holy fire in the mind of Martin Luther.

The message of Habakkuk is further evidence of the unity of God's Word. Salvation by faith, not works, is a key theme throughout both the Old and New Testaments. Though our works demonstrate our faith in and gratitude to God, we are justified not by works of the Law, but by faith. If we persevere in faith, God will eventually answer all of our troubling "Why?" questions.

Zephaniah: The Remnant of Israel

The book of Zephaniah is God's response to Judah's stubborn and idolatrous rejection of Him. Judah has already seen how God judged the northern kingdom of Israel by sending the Assyrians to conquer it and take the Israelites captive. Yet the wayward leaders and the people persist in their worship of Baal and Molek.

Zephaniah follows the Lord's thunderings against Judah with equally harsh pronouncements against the pagan nations that surround and threaten the nation.

Yet the book closes on a note of hope and the promise of a bright future. God will preserve a faithful remnant who love and serve the Lord:

> "But I will leave within you
> the meek and humble.
> The remnant of Israel
> will trust in the name of the LORD.
> They will do no wrong;
> they will tell no lies.
> A deceitful tongue
> will not be found in their mouths.
> They will eat and lie down
> and no one will make them afraid." (Zephaniah 3:12–13)

Zephaniah speaks of God's jealous wrath and unfailing love. God is not willing to share His people with false gods.

The aforementioned books of the "minor" prophets were all written before Judah was conquered and the Jews were led into Babylonian captivity. The next three books of the "minor" prophets—Haggai, Zechariah, and Malachi—were written after the Jews returned from exile.

Haggai: Time to Rebuild

The book of Haggai consists of two chapters, written around 530 BC, just before construction began on the new Temple. God speaks through Haggai, saying, "These people say, 'The time has not yet come to rebuild the Lord's house.'" The prophet then delivers God's response: "Is it a time for you yourselves to be living in your paneled houses, while [God's Temple] remains a ruin?"

God sent Haggai to remind the people that prosperity and blessing are gifts from God. Those who put their own selfish interests ahead of God's commands will lose His blessings. The theme of the book of Haggai is God's promise of abundant blessing for those who put Him first in their lives.

Zechariah: The King Is Coming!

Zechariah was written around the same time as Haggai. It is sometimes compared to Revelation because it opens with a series of apocalyptic visions. Zechariah reveals that the coming Messiah will not appear as a mighty king in royal robes, seated on a warhorse. Instead (in a prophecy of the Lord's arrival in Jerusalem on Palm Sunday), He will come humbly, a man of lowly birth, riding on a donkey:

> Rejoice greatly, Daughter Zion!
> Shout, Daughter Jerusalem!
> See, your king comes to you,
> righteous and victorious,
> lowly and riding on a donkey,
> on a colt, the foal of a donkey.
> (Zechariah 9:9)

Near the end, God speaks of the future day of the Lord, when all the nations that seek to destroy His people will themselves be consumed—and the whole world will know that the crucified Jesus is the glorified Lord over all:

> "On that day I will set out to destroy all the nations that attack Jerusalem. And I will pour out on the house of David and the inhabitants of Jerusalem a spirit of grace and supplication. They will look on Me, the one they have pierced, and they will mourn for Him as one mourns for an only child, and grieve bitterly for Him as one grieves for a firstborn son." (Zechariah 12:9–10)

Zechariah also contains this prophecy of the return of Jesus the Messiah to bring the final war to a close:

> Then the LORD will go out and fight against those nations, as He fights on a day of battle. On that day His feet will stand on the Mount of Olives, east of Jerusalem, and the Mount of Olives will be split in two from east to west, forming a great valley, with half of the mountain moving north and half moving south....Then the LORD my God will come, and all the holy ones with Him....It will be a unique day—a day known only to the LORD—with no distinction between day and night. When evening comes, there will be light.
>
> On that day living water will flow out from Jerusalem... (Zechariah 14:3–5, 7–8)

The prophecy of Zechariah is the promise of God's protection through the upheaval of the last days—and the promise of ultimate victory.

Malachi: The Sun of Righteousness

Malachi is the last book of the Old Testament. It opens with the words, "A prophecy: The word of the LORD to Israel through Malachi." In Hebrew, "Malachi" means "My messenger." So we don't know for certain if Malachi wrote it or if an unknown author identifies himself as God's messenger.

Much of Malachi is in the form of questions and answers. God says to the people, "I have loved you." The people respond, "How have you loved us?" And God goes back into the history of Jacob and Esau and explains His love for the Jews. The book contains warnings against breaking the sacrificial laws, defiling the Temple with false religious rites, sinning against one another, and breaking marriage vows.

The last two chapters are rich in prophetic content. In chapter 3, Malachi gives us a glimpse of the arrival of Jesus the Messiah, heralded by John the Baptist:

"I will send My messenger, who will prepare the way before Me. Then suddenly the Lord you are seeking will come to His temple; the messenger of the covenant, whom you desire, will come," says the LORD Almighty. (Malachi 3:1)

Then, in chapter 4, Malachi searches into the future, to the Day of Judgment, the day of the Second Coming of the Lord:

"Surely the day is coming; it will burn like a furnace. All the arrogant and every evildoer will be stubble, and the day that is coming will set them on fire," says the LORD Almighty. "Not a root or a branch will be left to them. But for you who revere My name, the sun of righteousness will rise with healing in its rays. And you will go out and frolic like well-fed calves." (Malachi 4:1–2)

We still await the dawning of the Sun of Righteousness, who will return with healing in His rays. He will shed light on our darkness and restore our sight. That is the good news of Malachi.

Four Centuries of Silence

Malachi was followed by four hundred years of silence—four centuries during which not a single word of Scripture was written. Those four hundred years form a gap between the Old and New Testaments. Theologians refer to this gap as "the intertestamental period."

Even though no Scripture was recorded during those years, history marched on. During the Persian Era, 450 to 330 BC, the Persian Empire controlled Judah. Though the Jews had limited self-rule and religious freedom, they were ultimately subject to the Persian authorities. From 334 to 324 BC, Alexander the Great conquered the Achaemenid Persian Empire, and the Jews came under Greek control. Many Jews adopted the Greek culture, which is why the New Testament was written in Greek. In 63 BC, the Roman general Pompey conquered Palestine and captured Jerusalem, and Judea came under Roman rule, which is why Jesus was tried and crucified by the Roman provincial government.

Prophecies Made, Promises Kept

The prophecies of the coming Messiah begin in the early pages of Genesis. They continue to appear here and there throughout the early books of the Old Testament. In the books of the prophets, Isaiah through Malachi, the predictions of the Messiah become much more precise and richly detailed. By the time we reach the end of the Old Testament, we have a very clear and multifaceted picture of what the promised Messiah will be like and how we can recognize Him. And yet the full identity of the Messiah awaits us in the next Testament, the New Testament.

A mysterious feature of the Old Testament is the amount of blood. Rivers of blood. Again and again, we see the sacrifice of animals, the spilling of blood. It begins when God slays animals to provide clothing for Adam and Eve. We see the spilling of animal blood in Abel's acceptable sacrifice to God. In Exodus, we see the blood of lambs splashed over the door at the first Passover. In Leviticus and beyond, God sets forth a system of rites and blood sacrifices to cleanse the people from their sins.

This river of blood flows throughout the Old Testament. Countless thousands of animals are sacrificed, and all this spilled blood seems to mean something—but what?

As we cross from the Old Testament to the New, light breaks through! A spotlight shines upon the One who was merely a silhouette in the Old Testament.

The first words of the New Testament announce: "This is the genealogy of Jesus the Messiah the son of David, the son of Abraham." Now we know the *name* of the Person the Old Testament has spoken of—and the New Testament links Him to the Old Testament with a genealogy that names Him "the son of David, the son of Abraham."

Jesus the Messiah fulfills the Old Testament prophecies. His death explains the Old Testament blood sacrifices. The Old Testament enables us to understand Jesus, and Jesus enables us to understand the Old Testament. As one New Testament writer explains:

> In the past God spoke to our ancestors through the prophets at many times and in various ways, but in these last days He has spoken to us by His Son, whom He appointed heir of all things, and through whom also He made the universe. (Hebrews 1:1–2)

During that four-hundred-year gap between the Old Testament and the New, the world held its breath, awaiting the birth of the Messiah. The story of the Old Testament is that the Messiah is coming. The story of the New Testament is that He has come. He lived and taught the people, died for our sins, and rose from the dead. And He is coming again.

13

Promises Kept:
Prophecies of the Coming King

A vi Loeb is an Israeli-American astrophysicist and the longest-serving chairman of Harvard University's astronomy department. On a popular podcast, Loeb talked about how one of the key features of the scientific method is "testability." In other words, if a scientist makes a claim, that claim can be tested. Scientists around the world can conduct experiments to either confirm or falsify the claim.

Then Loeb made a fascinating statement: not only can you conduct experiments to test *scientific* ideas, but you can conduct "an experimental test of theology."

He told a story attributed to the Jewish philosopher Martin Buber. "The story goes that Martin Buber said, 'The Christians argue that Jesus the Messiah has already arrived and will come back again in the future. The Jews argue that the Messiah never came and He will arrive in the future. So why argue? Both sides agree that the Messiah will arrive in the future. When the Messiah arrives, we can ask whether He visited us before. Then we can know.' This is an experimental test of theology. Even theology, if it puts skin in the game by making a prediction, can be tested."[1]

This is a profound statement, coming from one of the greatest scientific minds in the world today. In fact, the "experimental test of theology" that Loeb proposes has already been conducted hundreds of times in the pages of the Old Testament. God's Word has put "skin in the game" by making many predictions that can be—and have been—tested.

From Genesis to Malachi, the Old Testament contains hundreds of prophecies of a future Covenant, a future Kingdom, and a coming Messiah. Though many Old Testament prophecies will not be fulfilled until Jesus returns at the end of history, many were already fulfilled with astonishing precision during His earthly lifetime more than two thousand years ago.

Prophecies of the Coming Messiah

Again and again throughout the Old Testament, God speaks prophetically of a descendant of Abraham, Isaac, Jacob, and David—a descendant through whom all the people of the world will be blessed. The Old Testament predicted that this descendant, the Messiah, would be born of the specific lineage, in a specific way, in a specific place, at a specific time.

In Genesis 12:3, God promised Abraham that all the inhabitants of the world would be blessed through his lineage: "I will bless those who bless you, and whoever curses you I will curse; and all peoples on earth will be blessed through you." God reaffirmed this promise in Genesis 17:19 and 28:14.

In the earliest days of the Church, soon after the resurrected Lord ascended into Heaven, the Apostle Peter stood in the Temple and told the Jewish people that God's promise to Abraham was now fulfilled:

> "Indeed, beginning with Samuel, all the prophets who have spoken have foretold these days. And you are heirs of the prophets and of the covenant God made with your fathers. He said to Abraham, 'Through your offspring all peoples on earth will be blessed.' When God raised up his servant, he sent him first to you to bless you by turning each of you from your wicked ways." (Acts 3:24–26)

In Genesis 49, Jacob, the grandson of Abraham, called his sons to his deathbed to bless and prophesy about them. To his son Judah, the father of the Judean people, he said, "The scepter will not depart from Judah, nor the ruler's staff from between his feet, until He to whom it belongs shall come and the obedience of the nations shall be His" (Genesis 49:10). This is a prophecy of the Messiah, the coming Ruler whom all the nations will obey.

This is a strange prophecy, because it says that the scepter—the ruler's staff of authority—will not depart from Judah until the Ruler arrives. Why would the scepter of authority depart from Judah at the time of the Messiah's appearing? Wouldn't it make more sense that the Messiah would seize the scepter and wield it as the sign of His authority?

From the day Jacob pronounced that prophecy, the people of the tribe of Judah remained proudly unified and certain of their right to self-rule. After King Solomon died, the nation of Israel split into two kingdoms.

Even when the Babylonians destroyed Jerusalem and took the people of Judah into exile, the tribe remained united and determined to maintain their tribal authority and identity. The tribe of Judah was later returned to the land of Judah by Cyrus of Persia.

The symbolic scepter of self-rule that Jacob had promised did remain in the House of Judah for the next few centuries, even after Palestine came under Roman rule. The Romans permitted the Jews to maintain a great deal of self-rule, albeit under Roman supervision, through Herod the Great, the client-king of Judea.

In 4 BC, Herod the Great died, and his son, Herod Archelaus, became king of Samaria, Judea, and Idumea. In AD 6 the Roman emperor Caesar Augustus removed Herod Archelaus as king and made Judaea a province of Rome. At that moment, the scepter of self-rule departed from Judah. Many of the Jewish religious leaders were in despair. Why? The prophecy seemed to have failed. Where was the Messiah?

What no one knew at the time was that the Messiah had already come. He was a ten-year-old boy named Jesus, living in the Galilean town of Nazareth. Jesus had fulfilled Jacob's prophecy to the letter. No one else could fulfill that prophecy except Jesus, because once the Romans removed the scepter from Judah, the window of time for fulfilling it was shut forever.

It is worth noting, too, that as the Roman soldiers prepared to crucify Jesus, they placed a crown of thorns on His head and a mock scepter of wood in His hand, taunting Him with shouts of "Hail, King of the Jews!" (see Matthew 27:27–31). The same Romans who had removed the symbolic scepter from the House of Judah returned it to the hands of the One who will one day return and wield the supreme authority in Heaven and Earth.

In 2 Samuel 7:12–13, the prophet Nathan prophesied over King David,

> "When your days are over and you rest with your ancestors, I will raise up your offspring to succeed you, your own flesh and blood, and I will establish his kingdom. He is the one who will build a house for My Name, and I will establish the throne of his kingdom forever."

Jesus, of course, is David's "own flesh and blood," a lineal descendant of him (see Matthew 1:1). When Jesus arrived, He announced that "the kingdom of God is in your midst" (see Luke 17:21). When He returns, He will establish the throne of His kingdom forever, as Nathan foretold.

Prophecies of the Messiah's Birth

In Isaiah 7:14, God spoke through the prophet Isaiah, who told King Ahaz of Judah, "Therefore the Lord himself will give you a sign: The virgin will conceive and give birth to a son, and will call him Immanuel." The fulfillment of this prophecy is found in Matthew 1:18–25 and Luke 1:26–38, the two gospel accounts of Jesus's virgin birth. Matthew's account explains,

> All this took place to fulfill what the Lord had said through the prophet: "The virgin will conceive and give birth to a son, and they will call him Immanuel" (which means "God with us"). (vv. 22–23)

Many prophetic passages have two interpretations—one for the present and one for the future. The prophecy of the virgin birth in Isaiah 7:14 is one of these dual-interpretation prophecies. In this passage, Isaiah tells King Ahaz of Judah that God has promised to destroy Judah's enemies. As a sign that this promise was true, Isaiah predicted that a virgin or young woman (in Hebrew, *almah*) would give birth to a child.

The Hebrew word *almah* occurs seven times in the Old Testament and is usually translated "virgin" in English. But the authoritative resource *A Hebrew and English Lexicon of the Old Testament* by Brown, Driver, and Briggs states that *almah* can also mean a newly married young woman.

So when God, through Isaiah, told Ahaz to look for the sign of a young woman (*almah*) with a child named Immanuel, there was probably nothing miraculous about the child's birth. The boy Immanuel who was a sign to King Ahaz was undoubtedly conceived and born in the normal biological way to a young married mother in Israel. Isaiah never tells us what became of the young woman and young Immanuel—their story remains hidden from our view.

History only records one genuine virgin birth, and that is the birth of Jesus—which was the second and more important interpretation of Isaiah's prophecy. This more profound fulfillment would not be understood until after Jesus was miraculously born.

A complete list of all the messianic prophecies that were fulfilled in Jesus Christ would be too long for this book. As we noted earlier, Bible scholar Alfred Edersheim identified 456 Old Testament verses that Jewish rabbis viewed as messianic prophecies.[2] Let's take a brief overview of just a small number of them.

Prophecies of Messiah's Birth and Early Childhood

Micah 5:2 predicted that the Messiah would be born in Bethlehem; fulfilled in Matthew 2:4–6.

Hosea 11:1 predicted that the Messiah would be called out of Egypt as a child; fulfilled in Matthew 2:14–15.

Prophecies of Messiah's Forerunner, John the Baptist

Isaiah 40:3–4 promised that a forerunner would come to announce the Messiah; fulfilled by John the Baptist in Matthew 3, Mark 1, Luke 3, and John 1.

Malachi 4:5–6 promised that the Messiah's forerunner would come in the spirit of Elijah; fulfilled by John the Baptist in Matthew 11:10–15.

Prophecies of Messiah's Ministry

Moses, in Deuteronomy 18:15–16, predicted that God would raise up a prophet like Moses, an early prophecy of the Messiah; fulfilled in John 5:45–47.

In Exodus 12:5, the Old Testament sacrificial animals had to be unblemished as a symbol of the unblemished life of Jesus; fulfilled by Jesus in Hebrews 9:14. Also, compare Psalm 40:6–8 with Hebrews 10:5–10.

Psalm 78:1–2 predicted that Jesus would teach in parables; fulfilled by Jesus in Matthew 13:34–35.

Isaiah 6:9–10 predicted that the parables of Jesus would not be understood; fulfilled in Matthew 13:13–15.

Isaiah 35:5–6 predicted that the Messiah would perform miracles of healing; fulfilled in Matthew 11:2–6.

Isaiah 53:3 predicted that the Messiah would be a Suffering Servant, despised and rejected by those He came to save; fulfilled in Luke 4:28–29 and elsewhere.

Isaiah 8:14 pictured the coming Messiah as a stone that causes people to stumble; fulfilled in 1 Peter 2:7–8.

Isaiah 9:1–2 predicted that Messiah's ministry would begin in Galilee; fulfilled in Matthew 4:12–17.

Isaiah 11:10 promised that the Messiah would attract the nations to Himself; fulfilled in John 12:18–21, Acts 9:15, and elsewhere.

Zechariah 9:9 predicted that Jerusalem would rejoice to receive the Messiah as a King, riding upon a donkey; fulfilled by Jesus on the first Palm Sunday in Matthew 21:9, Mark 11:9, Luke 19:37–38, and John 12:13.

Prophecies of Messiah's Betrayal and Execution

More than twenty Old Testament prophecies were fulfilled within a mere twenty-four hours at the time of Jesus's crucifixion. Here are some of them:

Psalm 31:11 and Zechariah 13:7 predicted that Messiah would be abandoned by His friends; fulfilled in Mark 14:50.

Psalm 31:13 predicted that Messiah's enemies would conspire to kill Him; fulfilled in Matthew 27:1.

Isaiah 53:7 and Psalm 38:12–13 predicted that Messiah would not defend Himself before His accusers; fulfilled in Matthew 27:12–14.

The Passover ceremony described in Exodus 12:21–27 symbolizes the Messiah as our Passover Lamb; fulfilled by Jesus's death on the cross. See also 1 Corinthians 5:7.

Genesis 3:15 predicted that the Messiah would destroy Satan's work, crushing his head while suffering a wound in His heel; fulfilled in the crucifixion of Christ, as related in Matthew 27, Mark 15, Luke 23, and John 19; see also 1 John 3:8.

Psalm 41:9 predicted that Messiah would be betrayed by a close friend who shared His bread; fulfilled by Judas in John 13:18, 26–27.

Zechariah 11:12 predicted that the Messiah would be betrayed for thirty pieces of silver; fulfilled by Judas in Matthew 27:6–10.

Leviticus 17:11 specified blood sacrifices to make atonement for sin, a picture of the sacrifice of the Messiah; fulfilled by Jesus, who said, "This is My blood of the covenant, which is poured out for many for the forgiveness of sins" (Matthew 26:28).

Exodus 12:46 specified that none of the Passover lamb's bones should be broken, symbolizing the fact that Messiah's bones would not be broken when He was sacrificed; fulfilled in John 19:31–36.

Psalm 22:1 predicted that Messiah would be forsaken; fulfilled in Matthew 27:46 and Mark 15:34.

A thousand years before Roman crucifixion was invented, Psalm 22:16 predicted that Messiah's hands and feet would be pierced; fulfilled in Matthew 27:35, Mark 15:24, Luke 23:33, and John 19:18.

Psalm 22:15 predicted that the Messiah would suffer thirst; fulfilled in John 19:28.

Psalm 69:21 predicted that Messiah's executioners would offer him vinegar mingled with gall; fulfilled in Matthew 27:34.

Psalm 22:18 predicted that Messiah's executioners would cast lots for his clothing; fulfilled in John 19:23–24.

Psalm 31:5 prophesied the Messiah's last words before His death; fulfilled in Luke 23:46.

Prophecies of Messiah's Resurrection and Victory

Job 19:23–27, Psalm 16:9–11, and Psalm 118:17–18 predicted the Messiah's resurrection; fulfilled by the resurrection of Jesus in Matthew 28, Mark 16, Luke 24, and John 20.

Isaiah 25:7–8 prophesied that Messiah would destroy death; fulfilled in 1 Corinthians 15:54.

In 1 Samuel 2:35, Messiah is described as "a faithful priest" who will do the will of God; fulfilled in Hebrews 2:17.

Isaiah 44:3 prophesied that Messiah would pour out His Spirit on His people; fulfilled in John 20:22 and Acts 1:8.

Jeremiah 31:31 promised that Messiah would initiate a New Covenant between God and His people; fulfilled in Matthew 26:28.

Again, this is just a sampling of the many Old Testament prophecies that Jesus fulfilled. In Old Testament times, these prophecies baffled the scribes and religious teachers. They could not understand how the Messiah could be both a Suffering Servant and a conquering King of an everlasting Kingdom. Only with the benefit of hindsight and the record of the New Testament does it become clear that Jesus fulfilled all the prophecies of the Suffering Servant—and He will fulfill the prophecies of the conquering King when He returns.

The Compelling Gospel of the Old Testament Prophecies

In *The Case for Christ*, Lee Strobel presents an interview with Louis Lapides, a Jewish Christian scholar who has taught biblical studies at Biola University. Lapides was raised in a conservative Jewish family where the name of Jesus was never spoken (he was taught that Jesus was a "god of the Gentiles"). He grew up with the impression that the New Testament was "a handbook on anti-Semitism: how to hate Jews."

In the 1960s, Lapides was drafted and sent to Vietnam. He survived the war, but searched for meaning in marijuana, LSD, and Eastern religion—and he was even tempted for a while toward Satanism. In 1969, Lapides got into a discussion about God with a Los Angeles street preacher. The preacher gave him a Bible and challenged him to read it for himself.

Being Jewish, Lapides was reluctant to accept the challenge. "I'll read the Old Testament," he said, "but I'm not going to open up the other one."

"Fine," the preacher said. "Just read the Old Testament and ask the God of Abraham, Isaac, and Jacob—the God of Israel—to show you if Jesus is the Messiah."

He began reading the Old Testament—and when he got to Isaiah 53, he was shocked. The entire chapter was an unmistakable description of a Messiah who would suffer and die for the sins of the world. Isaiah's description of Jesus was so detailed and perfect that Lapides suspected Christians had tampered with the Old Testament text. So he obtained a Jewish Bible and read its translation of Isaiah 53— it was identical in its description of the suffering Messiah.

Lapides continued reading all the prophecies of the Messiah throughout the Old Testament, and was forced to his knees. On a trip to the Mojave Desert with friends, he went out alone and prayed, "God, I accept Jesus into my life. I don't understand what I'm supposed to do with Him, but I want Him."[3]

The prophecies of Jesus in the Old Testament are so numerous, specific, and compelling that a Jewish unbeliever can be led to Christ purely by reading them. As Scottish minister Alexander McLaren (1826–1910) observed, "Great tracts of Scripture are dark to us till life explains them, and then they come on us with the force of a new revelation."[4] So it is with the Old Testament prophecies that Jesus fulfilled.

PART V

The Kingdom of God and the New Covenant

What were shadows in the Old Testament have become brilliantly illuminated in the New Testament. The unnamed Messiah of the Old Testament is revealed to be Jesus of Nazareth, the Son of the Living God. The old fallen kingdom of Israel has been exchanged for the new and eternal Kingdom of God. The Old Covenant that was powerless to save has been exchanged for the New Covenant in Christ's saving blood. Old things have passed away. Behold, all things have become new!

14

The Suffering Servant
and the Kingdom

Oliver Cromwell was a military and political leader in Great Britain who experienced a dramatic conversion in his late twenties and became a devoted Christian. He once wrote in a letter, "Blessed be His Name for shining upon so dark a heart as mine!... O the riches of His mercy!"[1]

Cromwell believed God had called him to be a godly leader, and he served as Lord Protector of Great Britain from 1653 until his death on September 3, 1658. Lying on his deathbed at age fifty-nine, Cromwell called his wife and grown children around him and told them that the Covenant of God "is holy and true.... Love not the world. No, my children, live like Christians. I leave you the Covenant to feed upon."[2]

Cromwell's last thoughts and dying words were about the New Covenant of the blood of Jesus.

As we transition from the Old Testament to the New, it's as if someone flicks on a dazzling halogen lamp. Suddenly, everything that was dark and shadowy in the Old Testament comes into brilliant focus. The mysterious Old Testament prophecies of a coming Kingdom and a New Covenant are embodied in a Person.

And the name of that Person is Jesus of Nazareth.

The Suffering Servant in the Old and New Testaments

Jewish scribes and teachers in Old Testament times admitted being baffled by the prophecies of Isaiah 53, which described a "Suffering Servant" who would be "despised and rejected by mankind" and "pierced for our transgressions" and "led like a lamb to the slaughter." Finally, Isaiah says that the Suffering Servant would be raised from the dead: "After He has suffered, He will see the light of life and be satisfied" (Isaiah 53:11). These prophecies are so detailed and precise, it's as if Isaiah wrote a biography of Jesus some seven hundred years before He came and lived it.

The prophecy of the Suffering Servant in Isaiah highlights the truly unexpected, even paradoxical nature of the Kingdom of God. It is not an earthly kingdom established on military triumphs, like the Roman Empire or the Persian Empire or Alexander the Great's kingdom of Macedon. No, the Kingdom of God is established through the humiliation, suffering, and death of its King. God confounds human expectations by establishing His Kingdom through the Suffering Servant.

But the suffering of the Messiah is only the beginning of the establishment of the Kingdom. The pathway to His triumph leads through suffering. Both the suffering and the victory are foretold throughout the Old Testament.

Isaiah describes this Servant in many passages. He will bring light and liberty to the Gentiles (Isaiah 42:6–7). He will intercede with God's own Spirit (Isaiah 42:1). He will proclaim the good tidings of God's redemption (Isaiah 61:1–3). He intercedes with God day and night for the victory of His purpose (Isaiah 62:1, 6). He willingly accepts His mission, though it is certain to bring Him suffering (Isaiah 50:4–5).

This was a strange and troubling concept to the Jews, who associated suffering and death with the curse of sin. How could the Messiah suffer and die like a common sinner?

Under the inspiration of the Holy Spirit, Isaiah gazed into the very mystery of the Godhead to receive the answer: God does not save the human race through ritual atonement or the strict observance of the Law. No, He redeems the human race through the suffering of His Servant. In the prophecies of Isaiah, the Old Testament leaps forward in time and links arms with the New Testament.

The Servant is the personification of the true Israel. Though the nation of Israel was rebellious, the Servant, the true Israel, will be obedient to God's calling (see Isaiah 49:1–6). All that the true Israel was and is converges in Him.

The Suffering Servant is the "new Moses" that God promised through Moses in Deuteronomy 18:15: "The Lord your God will raise up for you a prophet like me from among you, from your fellow Israelites. You must listen to him." This new Moses will be the true and loyal Israel and the leader of His people. All of these promises are fulfilled in Jesus of Nazareth.

The Mission of Jesus, the Suffering Servant

The Suffering Servant of Isaiah is interpreted differently in Judaism and in Christianity. In Judaism, the Suffering Servant represents the nation of Israel. In Christianity, the Suffering Servant is a literal Person, Jesus the Messiah. In both Judaism and Christianity, He fulfills two roles—prophet and priest.

As a prophet, the Suffering Servant brings God's message of comfort, healing, peace, and salvation to the people. He prophetically proclaims God's righteousness to the world.

As a priest, the Suffering Servant makes atonement for the people's sins by taking upon Himself the punishment they deserve for sin. In this role, He cleanses the people of their guilt and restores their relationship with God. In fact, we can parse the word atonement to mean "at-one-ment." The Suffering Servant, our High Priest, removes our guilt so that we can be "at one" with God.

You and I, as followers of Christ, are the "new Israel." As disciples of the Suffering Servant, we are called to follow His example and do what He did. We are called to be prophets, proclaiming God's righteousness to the world. We are called to be priests, leading people to God so they can find forgiveness, redemption, and salvation through Jesus, the crucified and risen Lord.

In the ancient Jewish view, suffering always follows sin. But Isaiah presented an entirely new view of the problem of pain. Suffering, he said, is often a direct result of doing God's will. No longer is suffering mere agony without meaning. Instead, God can transform suffering into His chosen instrument of redemption. Through it, we can enter the very character of God's Servant and share in His redemptive purpose. The Jews did not want a Messiah who suffers. They wanted a triumphant Messiah. And are we any different? Are we willing to suffer with Him for the Gospel of the Kingdom? Or do we want Jesus to give us a life of ease?

His Mission Is Our Mission

In the fullness of time, the Servant came to announce (quoting the messianic passage in Isaiah 61:1–2):

> "The Spirit of the Lord is on me,
> because he has anointed me
> to proclaim good news to the poor.
> He has sent me to proclaim freedom for the prisoners
> and recovery of sight for the blind,
> to set the oppressed free,
> to proclaim the year of the Lord's favor." (Luke 4:18–19)

Then He rolled up the scroll of Isaiah and said, "Today this Scripture is fulfilled in your hearing." God had promised Abraham, "All peoples on earth will be blessed through you." Jesus the Servant, a descendant of Abraham, was the fulfillment of that ancient promise.

Israel did occasionally make proselytes, welcoming non-Jews into its community of faith. But on the whole, Judaism never became a missionary religion as God intended. Instead, the people tended to draw ever more tightly into themselves.

So Jesus manifested a new Israel, a true Israel, after His resurrection when He told His disciples:

> "All authority in heaven and on earth has been given
> to Me. Therefore go and make disciples of all nations,
> baptizing them in the name of the Father and of the
> Son and of the Holy Spirit, and teaching them to obey

everything I have commanded you. And surely I am with
you always, to the very end of the age."
(Matthew 28:18–20)

The Servant is revealed to be the King, with all authority in
Heaven and on Earth. Now He sends us out to make disciples.

So we must ask ourselves: Do we really understand what it
means to serve the Suffering Servant? Do we take this calling seriously? Are we willing to suffer with Him in order to carry out the
commission He gave us?

Or do we merely want a Jesus who is enshrined in stained-glass
images and stained-glass doctrines? Do we want a Jesus who asks
nothing of us, who is our Savior but not our Lord? A Jesus who
lays down His life so that we might live in comfort and ease? That
is not the Jesus of the Bible. That is not the Jesus who has called us
into His Kingdom.

The Jesus of the Bible calls us to take up our cross and follow
Him. He calls us to lose our lives in order to find life. He calls us to
pray, "Your Kingdom come, Your will be done." We cannot take
part in the Kingdom of the Servant unless we are willing to follow
the Servant, and pattern our lives after His.

In our culture, we see churches that preach "gospels" of prosperity or political power, churches that seem to welcome only one
ethnic community, churches that are unwilling to serve the poor
and outcasts, and churches that seem to draw a line between "us"
and "them." Meanwhile, most of the world is sliding into eternity
without Jesus.

We say that advancing the Kingdom of God is our first
priority—but can the people around us see our Kingdom values in
the way we run our businesses, use our money, or show hospitality

to strangers? Do we, in our churches and homes, draw boundary lines between ourselves and the world? Do we hang a "Do Not Disturb" sign on our church doors in order to restrict membership in the Kingdom to people who meet our strict approval?

Ancient Israel was not a welcoming kingdom. It did not preach the good news of Yahweh to neighboring tribes. It did not invite foreigners to join in worshiping the one true God. Have we in the Church become an exclusive club like that?

The church that seeks to restrict its membership and keep out the "riffraff" is not following the Servant. It is merely worshiping a small, strange god made in its own image.

God's Kingdom Is Universal

It is possible for a church, or any group of Christians, to become exclusionary simply through fear of contamination. This is exactly why Israel became an insular, isolated culture that made no effort to proclaim Yahweh to the surrounding nations. In such an atmosphere, the Israelites could not understand and accept the Suffering Servant's mission.

From the beginning of the Old Testament, we read that the scope of God's rule is universal (Genesis 1:1; Isaiah 54:5; Jeremiah 32:27). He is the only true, eternal, and living God, and all nations are invited to worship Him (Psalm 117:1), not just Israelites. Non-Jews (often called "strangers") were treated with kindness and legal rights under the Law (see Exodus 20:10; Leviticus 16:29, 17:8, 19:34; and Deuteronomy 1:6, 10:18, 14:29, 16:14, 24:17–19).

God, through Isaiah, called all the nations, from all corners of the earth, to turn to Him and be saved (Isaiah 45:22–23). He appointed Israel, His servant kingdom, to shine the light of His salvation to all nations and peoples (Isaiah 49:6; 51:4–5). And let's not forget the example of Jonah, the reluctant prophet God sent to Nineveh to call the Assyrian people to repentance. God intended him to be one among many Israelite missionaries who would take His message to the nations, but Jonah exemplified the Israelite mindset: *Why should Gentiles repent and be saved? Aren't the Gentile nations our enemies? Aren't they idolaters? Haven't the Gentiles killed countless Israelites? Why would we want to bring them into the Kingdom of God?*

The thought of allowing the Gentiles full participation in the Kingdom, Covenant, and worship of God was not popular in Israel. In order for God to enlarge the Kingdom to encompass the entire world, He would have to use other means.

15

The Gospels:
Four Storytellers, One Story

Jerome of Stridon was a Christian theologian in a time of persecution. Born in the Roman province of Dalmatia, he is best known for translating the Hebrew Old Testament and Greek New Testament into Latin (his translation is known as the Vulgate edition, meaning "in the common tongue"). A wealthy Roman nobleman, as well as a devout Christian, Jerome moved to Palestine so he could visit the places he read and wrote about in his Bible translations.

On Christmas Eve, just after he had finished his translation of the Bible, the Lord Jesus appeared to Jerome in a dream and said, "What will you give Me for My birthday?"

Jerome eagerly replied, "Lord, I will give You my translation of Your Word."

Jesus said, "No, Jerome, that's not what I want."

Jerome was disappointed. He had labored over his translation for four decades—yet here was Jesus, telling him He wanted something else. Jerome asked, "What else can I give You? Should I give You all my possessions?"

Jesus said, "No, I don't want any of those things."

"Should I give You all my money?"

"No, I don't want your money."

"Tell me, Lord! What would give You joy on your birthday? What can I give You?"

Jesus said, "Give Me all your sins."[1]

The essential message of the gospels is that Jesus came to take all our sins, from root to fruit. The root of sin is our fallen nature, which we inherited from our first parents, Adam and Eve. The fruit of sin is all the ways we say to God, "I will not surrender my will to You!" This is expressed in our selfishness as well as in our addictions, anger, bitterness, lust, jealousy, envy, pride, judgmentalism, self-pity, lovelessness, dishonesty, and more. Jesus's message to us is the same as His message to Jerome: "Give Me all your sins."

The Kingdom of God Has Come Near

The four gospels—Matthew, Mark, Luke, and John—are four accounts of the life, death, and resurrection of Jesus the Messiah. Evangelical scholars believe they were written between AD 50 and 90. The Gospel of Mark is considered the earliest.

Matthew, Mark, and Luke are the three "synoptic Gospels" (from the Greek *synoptikos*, which means "seen together"). They largely parallel each other in the way they tell the gospel story, though with interesting differences.

The Gospel of Matthew appears to be intended for Hellenized (Greek-speaking) Jewish Christians. Mark's gospel, with its explanations of certain Jewish customs, seems to be aimed at a Gentile Christian audience. Luke's gospel is addressed to "Theophilus," which means "Lover of God," so it may be addressed to a person by that name or to all Christians who truly love God. Matthew was written by the disciple and former tax collector Matthew, also called Levi. Mark was written by John Mark, the Apostle Peter's close friend, whom he called "my son Mark" in 1 Peter 5:13. Luke's gospel was written by a Gentile named Luke, a missionary companion of the Apostle Paul and (according to Colossians 4:14) a doctor. Luke also wrote a sequel, the book of Acts. He was not an eyewitness to the life of Jesus, but he "carefully investigated everything from the beginning" in order to "write an orderly account" (Luke 1:3).

The Gospel of John was written by the Apostle John (who identifies himself in the text several times as "the disciple whom Jesus loved"). John's beautifully poetic tone contrasts markedly with the almost journalistic style of the three synoptic gospels. His purpose is not to summarize the life and ministry of Jesus, but to make the case for His identity as the Messiah.

Unlike the synoptic gospels, John does not mention Jesus's ancestry, birth, baptism, temptation, or transfiguration. He arranges some incidents in a different order than the synoptics, and makes it clear that the length of Jesus's earthly ministry was three years.

The word "gospel" is an English translation of the Greek word *euangelion* ("good news"). In Old English, the term for "good news" was *gōdspel* (*gōd*, meaning "good" and *spel*, meaning "news"). The word *gōdspel* eventually became "gospel."

The differences between the gospels do not mean there is disagreement between them. Though the authors of the four gospels wrote from four points of view, they present one unified message: The prophecies are fulfilled. The long-awaited Messiah has come.

They tell us that Jesus the Messiah did mighty works, preached the Good News of the Kingdom, was crucified, and rose again. This Jesus now lives and has been exalted to the highest Heaven, where He sits at the right hand of God. On a day known only to God the Father, He will return to judge the living and the dead, and bring history to a close.

Jesus introduced His ministry with these words: "The time has come. The kingdom of God has come near. Repent and believe the good news!" (Mark 1:15). In Him, the unity of all Scripture is plainly presented. Through Him the two Testaments are inextricably linked. All biblical theology revolves around Him.

New Wine and Old Wineskins

The Old Testament has one overarching theme: the people of God, the nation of Israel. But an underlying theme also runs through the Old Testament: the coming Messiah. It is less obvious, but it is pervasive from Genesis to Malachi. The Old Testament by itself is incomplete. The New Testament without the Old Testament does not make sense. They are two halves of a complete whole. The Old Testament feels like a story whose ending the author hasn't yet written, or like a mystery novel with the last few chapters torn out. If the Bible had ended at Malachi, we would get to the end and say, "That's it? What happens next?"

But thank God, the story does not end with Malachi. We turn the page to the New Testament and find that Jesus is the realization of all that the prophets had promised and hoped for. The Kingdom of God had finally come near.

Even though there is a profound unity that binds the Old and New Testaments together, there is also a major difference between the two Testaments. For obvious reasons, the personality of Jesus the Messiah looms large over the New Testament. We immediately see Him wading into conflict with legalistic Judaism. His teachings and actions explode its rigid rules and requirements like a rapidly fermenting new wine poured into stiff old wineskins. As Jesus Himself said:

> "And no one pours new wine into old wineskins. Otherwise, the wine will burst the skins, and both the wine and the wineskins will be ruined. No, they pour new wine into new wineskins." (Mark 2:22)

Even though the gospel of salvation by grace through faith lies at the heart of the Old Testament, its truths had been painted over by all the legalistic rules the scribes and Pharisees instituted. So Jesus came to shatter the hard shell of legalism that had grown up around God's Old Testament truth. That's why He declares: "Do not think that I have come to abolish the Law or the Prophets; I have not come to abolish them but to fulfill them" (Matthew 5:17).

The people of Israel expected the Messiah to restore their political sovereignty and overthrow Roman rule. This hope was especially strong in a Jewish political faction known as the Zealots. Judas Iscariot, who betrayed Jesus, was a probably a member of this party. Some Bible scholars point to his surname, Iscariot, as a form of the title *Sicarii*, meaning "dagger-men," a label for a band of violent ultra-Zealots who sometimes carried out assassinations.

Act One and Act Two

Many first-century Jews rejected Christ, but those who followed Him became the nucleus of a new way of life called the Church. While the Old Testament is concerned with the fortunes of the people of Israel, the New Testament broadens from that limited landscape to a new and universal horizon.

We must be careful not to say (as some do) that the New Testament is all we need, that we can safely dispense with the Old Testament. And we must also avoid the heretical notion that the Old Testament reveals a God of wrath but the New Testament shows us a God of love. He is consistently shown to be a God of both justice and grace throughout both Testaments.

At the same time, we must not minimize the supremacy of the New Testament revelation. In Galatians 3:24–35, Paul contrasts the Old Testament Law with the New Testament revelation of faith in Jesus Christ:

> So the law was our guardian until Christ came that we might be justified by faith. Now that this faith has come, we are no longer under a guardian.

And the writer to the Hebrews tells us that Jesus's priestly ministry is superior to sacrifices made by the priests in Old Testament times:

> But in fact the ministry Jesus has received is as superior to theirs as the covenant of which He is mediator is superior to the old one, since the new covenant is established on better promises. (Hebrews 8:6)

Jesus and His disciples were Jews who did not think they were founding a new religion. They were fulfilling the promises and demands of the Old Testament. Though the Gospel was universal in its scope, available to Jew and Gentile alike, Jesus viewed His mission as being focused, first of all, to "the lost sheep of Israel" (see Matthew 10:6 and 15:24). The New Testament is truly the fulfillment of Israel's greatest hope.

In the Old Testament, the rule of God is always cast in the future tense. "The days are coming," warn the prophets Jeremiah, Hosea, and Amos. "In that day," warn many Old Testament prophets, notably Isaiah.

But in the New Testament, we encounter a dramatic change in the language. The writers switch from future tense to present tense: "The kingdom of God has come upon you" (Matthew 12:28). "The secret of the Kingdom of God has been given to you" (Mark 4:11). "Yours is the Kingdom of God" (Luke 6:20). "The Kingdom of God is being preached, and everyone is forcing their way into it" (Luke 16:16). "The Kingdom of God is in your midst" (Luke 17:21).

The Old and New Testaments stand together as two acts of a single drama. Act One points to its conclusion in Act Two. Without Act Two, the play is incomplete. But without Act One, it is impossible to fully understand the meaning of Act Two.

The "Intolerable" Claims of Jesus

Jesus expressed a profound truth when He said, "My kingdom is not of this world" (John 18:36). His concept of the Kingdom was not at all the popular notion.

Most Jews of that time were nurtured on the apocalyptic hope described in the book of Daniel, the hope of God's sudden intervention appearing from the sky:

> "In my vision at night I looked, and there before me was one like a son of man, coming with the clouds of heaven. He approached the Ancient of Days and was led into His presence. He was given authority, glory, and sovereign power; all nations and peoples of every language worshiped Him. His dominion is an everlasting dominion that will not pass away, and His Kingdom is one that will never be destroyed." (Daniel 7:13–14)

The Jews were not wrong to expect their Messiah to arrive among the clouds at some unknown future time. But that description in Daniel 7 applies to the Second Coming of the Messiah. At his first coming, Jesus arrived without heavenly fanfare. He Himself explained that His Second Coming would be very different from His first when He told the high priest, "And you will see the Son of Man sitting at the right hand of the Mighty One and coming on the clouds of heaven" (Mark 14:62).

This was Jesus's explicit claim to be the prophesied Messiah. And the dramatic miracle of the resurrection, attested to by many witnesses, confirmed it (Romans 1:3–4). He is the preexisting Son who emptied Himself and "made Himself nothing" to take human form and identify with us (Philippians 2:6–8). He is the very image of the substance of God, far above the angels, and He now sits at the right hand of the divine majesty (see Hebrews 1). He is the Word, the cosmic *Logos* who has existed since before the beginning of time and space (John 1:1–3).

These were intolerable claims to the first-century Jews (just as they are intolerable to Muslims today). The ancient world had seen many self-proclaimed "god-men," "divine kings," and "living messiahs" who clamored for attention among the pagans. The first-century Jews rightly abhorred such claims.

In fact, a century and a half before the birth of Christ, tens of thousands of Jews fought and died rather than bow down to Antiochus Epiphanes, a Hellenistic king of the Seleucid Empire who ruled over Jewish territory. Like many Hellenistic rulers, he claimed divine status (the incarnation of the Greek god Zeus), and demanded to be worshiped.

Many Jews were quite skeptical of—and offended by—anyone claiming to be God or godlike in any way. They were not expecting the promised Messiah to be God Himself—someone extraordinary, yes, who was God's anointed one, but still a mere human being. When Jesus came claiming to be not only the Messiah but the Son of God, the Jews could only interpret His words as blasphemy.

And when He was crucified and laid in the grave, they felt vindicated. If Jesus was truly the Messiah, they reasoned, He would not have allowed the crucifixion to take place. The true Messiah could have come down from the cross (Matthew 27:41–43).

Muslims agree with the Jews on this point, except they maintain that God could not and did not allow this good prophet (whom they call Isa ibn Maryam or "Isa, son of Mary") to suffer and die. The Quran states that Isa didn't die on the cross but was miraculously spared by God. As Paul declared, the cross is "a stumbling block to Jews and foolishness to Gentiles" (1 Corinthians 1:23).

Jesus the Messiah summons all people of all nations and ethnicities to become citizens of the Kingdom of God. Because it is the Kingdom of the Suffering Servant, it is a realm of the meek and lowly. Those who would lead in this Kingdom must be willing to "be the very last, and the servant of all" (Mark 9:35). Jesus set an example of serving for all believers to follow:

> When He had finished washing their feet, He put on His clothes and returned to His place. "Do you understand what I have done for you?" He asked them. "You call Me 'Teacher' and 'Lord,' and rightly so, for that is what I am. Now that I, your Lord and Teacher, have washed your feet, you also should wash one another's feet. I have set you an example that you should do as I have done for you." (John 13:12–15)

Those who would enter the Kingdom of God must endure suffering and persecution (Matthew 5;12; Luke 6:20–23). We cannot buy our way into the Kingdom. In fact, wealth and possessions actually keep many people from entering (Mark 10:17–25). The Kingdom belongs to those who shed all pride in their own righteousness, wisdom, accomplishments, or position. In fact, the Kingdom belongs to those who become as little children (Mark 10:14).

Entry into the Kingdom will probably not bring one public acclamation. In fact, it demands utter self-denial. Over and over, Jesus reminded His disciples—and us—that there is a tremendous cost to the Kingdom life. If the Kingdom demands it, a person must be ready to leave father and mother, home and family, at a moment's notice (Matthew 19:29; Mark 10:29; Luke 18:29). The world hates and persecutes the Kingdom and all who identify with it (Mark 13:13; Luke 6:22).

To be a citizen of the Kingdom means to be hated, but never to retaliate. When we are struck on one cheek, we turn the other to receive the next blow (Matthew 5:39). Those who heed the Kingdom summons have nothing to look forward to in this life but the cross and servitude (Matthew 10:38; Mark 8:34; Luke 14:27).

The Kingdom of God, Today and Tomorrow

What is the Kingdom of God like?

The Kingdom of God has no measurable boundaries. It is not a region of so many square miles of real estate. It is *people*. Specifically, it's the people who are called by God and who have submitted to His sovereign rule.

God invites every member of the human race to make a radical decision for the Kingdom of Christ—or against it. Those who heed the call have not merely *entered* the Kingdom; they *are* the Kingdom.

What are Kingdom citizens called to do? The most important task of the Church is to proclaim the Gospel, which is the Good News of salvation.

The modern world is in thrall to demonic powers. Everywhere we look, evil and injustice seem to triumph. But there is good news! The power of the cross has broken the power of Satan. The resurrection of Jesus Christ has launched the age of the New Covenant and the ascendancy of the Kingdom of God. Let men and women renounce their old allegiances to sin and self and begin a new life as citizens of the Kingdom.

This is the Gospel of Jesus Christ, and we have no other.

The preaching of the Gospel often seems to fall on deaf ears. Yet it is good news that fulfills humanity's deepest longings. Even when people are not aware that they need the saving message of the Kingdom, they still grope in the darkness for it.

Human beings can no more escape the longing for the Kingdom than they can escape themselves. It lies at the heart of human nature. People peer into the windows of the Kingdom of God but do not know how to enter, because Satan's agents of deception lure them away from the promise of salvation.

People are idolaters by nature. Though they long for God, they will settle for false idols. Though they long for the ecstasy of Heaven, they will settle for cheap earthly thrills. Though they long for eternity with God, they will settle for the temporary gratification of wealth, power, or fame. The false gods of the twenty-first century are as deceptive and deadly as the demon-god Baal in ancient Palestine.

Into this global morass of demonic deception, the Church of Jesus Christ proclaims the Gospel of the Kingdom. The Church places its hope squarely on the truth of the Bible because it knows no other truth. It announces the Kingdom of God as the goal of history and the only hope for man's redemption.

The Tension of the Kingdom

The Church's tension is that it is *in* the world but not *of* the world. The more seriously the Church takes its task, the more deeply estranged it becomes from this modern age. The bolder the Church's witness for Christ, the more it will be hated and persecuted. Like the persecuted first-century church, we are called upon to live in this tension—and to even provoke it through our witness for Jesus.

We are also in a tension between the Kingdom of God as an accomplished, present reality and its future victory. We know that

Jesus has already won the victory on the cross—yet we still expectantly await a final victory that we cannot see.

The early Church understood itself to be the successor of Israel, the true remnant and people of the New Covenant. The early Christians saw their mission as a servant mission of proclaiming the Kingdom and extending the Covenant to the world. They saw themselves as the people of the Messiah living in the Last Days.

We are the same Church, and we have the same Gospel. Our task is unchanged and our message has not lost its urgency. And we must live in a state of tension between the victory Jesus won on the cross and the victory that is still deferred.

Around the world, the invisible Church of Jesus Christ is quietly engaged in ministry, evangelism, and worship in house churches and secret cell meetings, hiding from the searching eyes of Communist regimes, Islamic regimes, and even hostile neighbors. Tension is inescapable. It is a tension between two worlds: the Kingdom of God victorious and the Church of Jesus Christ, hated and hunted and persecuted.

What will the Kingdom of God be tomorrow? What is the future of the Church?

The true Church is the invisible Church, consisting of everyone whose name is written in the Book of Life (see Revelation 20:12 and 21:27). It is greater than local church bodies and denominations, just as the true Israel of God's purpose was greater than the Israelite nation.

The true Church resides in every individual church, yet surpasses all of them. No one church may claim to be the "true Church" because that would be the sin of self-deification. The true Church cuts across the membership rolls of individual churches and reaches out to embrace repentant sinners. The true Church transcends time and space.

In the true Church—the true Kingdom of God—we will one day sit down with Father Abraham, the great apostles, and all the saved believers from every nation and race. The Church is the community of people who have responded in faith to the summons of the Kingdom of God.

The Church is the new Israel, the new people of God. And it has been called to action!

Our Missionary Calling

If the Church is the new Israel, then it has undertaken the very destiny and mission of Israel. This is no passive destiny, but rather a bold and challenging missionary calling. In fact, God calls us to be a missionary people. If it is not boldly witnessing to the world and making disciples, then it is not the Church.

Our Gospel declares that salvation lies only in the Kingdom of God. That's why Jesus began His ministry by announcing, "The time has come. The kingdom of God has come near. Repent and believe the good news!" (Mark 1:15). Our mission is His mission—to announce the Kingdom, call people to repentance and faith, and declare this salvation to the world.

God does not call the Church to merely state its message as an objective fact, take it or leave it. We are to summon men and women to Jesus and His Kingdom. We are to campaign for the souls of human beings. The Church is to capture men and women for the redemptive fellowship of the Kingdom of Christ.

The growth of the Kingdom cannot be measured by the statistical growth of visible churches. Those are the palest approximation of the Body of Christ. The voice of the visible church is often irrelevant and dull and inspires little confidence. The visible church may summon people—but to what is often hard to say.

While visible churches must not be the center of our devotion, we must still carry out the mission of the Kingdom through them. So the Church is called to be a people under God's rule who exhibit before the world the righteousness and selfless love of His Kingdom. As Jesus said, "As I have loved you, so you must love one another. By this everyone will know that you are my disciples, if you love one another" (John 13:34–35).

Paul tells us that God is "reconciling the world to himself in Christ, not counting people's sins against them. And he has committed to us the message of reconciliation" (2 Corinthians 5:19). Jesus is reconciling the world *through us*. What a responsibility! Jesus said, "Whoever wants to be My disciple must deny themselves and take up their cross and follow Me" (Mark 8:34). The cross is our path to victory. History tells us that God's people have achieved great things when they cast themselves straight into the teeth of history at their Master's command. But if we grow complacent, if we refuse to take up our cross and follow Him, we will become useless to God and humanity alike.

The world is growing dark and dangerous. We may be called upon to suffer and lose our lives for the sake of the Gospel and the Kingdom. May we face the uncertain future with the prayer Jesus taught us on our lips: "Your Kingdom come, Your will be done, on Earth as it is in Heaven."

16

The Parables:
Pictures of the Kingdom

On April 3, 1968, Dr. Martin Luther King Jr. delivered a speech at Mason Temple in Memphis, Tennessee, which has become known as "I've Been to the Mountaintop." In that speech, he spoke at length about Jesus's Parable of the Good Samaritan.

King recalled a visit to Israel with his wife. They rented a car and drove down the Jericho Road. As they drove, King realized the road was dangerous and "really conducive to ambushing." In the time of Jesus, King said, it was known as the Bloody Pass because of all the robberies and murders that occurred there.

The road begins in Jerusalem at an elevation of nearly 2,500 feet and twists, turns, and meanders down to Jericho, almost 850 feet below sea level. As King and his wife drove, he remarked, "I can see why Jesus used this as the setting for His parable."

> [Jesus] talked about a certain man, who fell among thieves. You remember that a Levite and a priest passed by on the other side. They didn't stop to help him. And finally a man of another race came by.... [He] got down with him, administered first aid, and helped the man in need. Jesus ended up saying, this was the good man, this was the great man, because he had the capacity to...be concerned about his brother. . . .
>
> The first question that the priest asked, the first question that the Levite asked was, "If I stop to help this man, what will happen to me?" But then the Good Samaritan came by and he reversed the question: "If I do not stop to help this man, what will happen to him?"[1]

The day after King delivered that speech, he was assassinated.

This ancient story by the Lord Jesus, the Parable of the Good Samaritan, has been widely used in countless situations and cultural contexts to make this point: *All* of us—both individually and collectively—have a duty to love our neighbors. It is a story that tells us how citizens of the Kingdom should behave toward their neighbors.

The parable tells us that we have a Kingdom duty to love and care for others despite religious or ethnic differences. It tells us that instead of worrying about the cost, we should leap into action to serve and save others. It tells us that Christian love places no limits on who our neighbor is.

The parables of Jesus have power to change lives and societies. The Parable of the Good Samaritan, for example, has been a moral touchstone and motivating factor in the abolition movement, the civil rights movement, the pro-life movement, the homelessness movement, and such humanitarian organizations as the Salvation

Army and Samaritan's Purse. One of its Kingdom implications is that God calls us to show love and kindness not merely to those who are already in the Kingdom, but to outsiders, strangers, and even enemies.

The Kingdom Parables

A parable is a simple, memorable story that teaches deep truths through word pictures and analogies and often ends with a surprise twist. The parables of Jesus are found in the synoptic gospels and comprise about a third of His teachings. The parables involved believable situations from everyday life but engaged the hearers' imaginations to make them memorable. For example, Jesus made a Samaritan—who was considered an outcast and an enemy of Jewish society—the hero of one parable. This image had considerable shock value among His hearers and forced them to think deeply about His message.

Jesus also used parables to unlock spiritual mysteries. Some deal with the power of prayer ("The Friend at Night," "The Unjust Judge," "The Pharisee and the Publican"), some with love and forgiveness ("The Good Samaritan," "The Unforgiving Servant"), and quite a few with salvation and the End Times ("The Ten Virgins," "The Rich Fool," "The Wheat and the Tares"). At least six of Jesus's parables are focused specifically on showing us, in vivid terms, what the Kingdom of God is like.

After telling His disciples the Parable of the Sower (Matthew 13, Mark 4, Luke 8), Jesus said, "To you it has been given to know the secrets of the kingdom of heaven." He began the Parable of the Hidden Treasure (Matthew 13) by saying, "The kingdom of heaven is like treasure hidden in a field." "The Pearl of Great Price" speaks of the immense value of the Kingdom.

The parables of the Growing Seed (Mark 4) and the Mustard Seed (Matthew 13, Mark 4, and Luke 13) speak of the rapid growth of the Kingdom from small, almost invisible beginnings, using the image of a tiny seed that grows into a large tree. The Parable of the Leaven (Matthew 13 and Luke 13) also points to the astounding growth of God's Kingdom. A tiny lump of yeast can cause a small mass of dough to multiply in volume—just as the Church began with Jesus and a dozen disciples and grew to number millions of followers down through the centuries and around the world. The Kingdom of God transforms and magnifies everything it touches.

If we truly want to understand the Good News of the Kingdom of God and peer into God's agenda for human history, the Lord's parables are an indispensable source of insight.

17

Acts:
Proclaiming and Expanding
the Kingdom

The book of Acts, Luke's sequel to his gospel, is the story of the founding of the Christian Church and the spread of the Kingdom message throughout the Roman Empire. Luke probably wrote it around AD 80 to 90.

Acts picks up where Luke's gospel leaves off: with the ascension of Jesus. Acts recaps the forty days that Jesus spent with the disciples before He was taken up into Heaven. In Acts 1, Luke tells us that, after His crucifixion and resurrection, Jesus appeared to the apostles and "gave many convincing proofs that He was alive. He appeared to them over a period of forty days and spoke about the kingdom of God."

The early Church eagerly began preaching the Good News of the Kingdom and the New Covenant that Jesus had entrusted to His followers. The first few chapters are set in Jerusalem and depict the coming of the Holy Spirit on the Day of Pentecost and the establishment of the early Church in Jerusalem.

The themes of the Kingdom of God and the Covenant are woven throughout the book. In Acts 3, Peter preaches in the Temple, showing from the Old Testament scriptures that the New Covenant has come, fulfilling God's Old Covenant promise to Abraham and the prophets:

> "Indeed, beginning with Samuel, all the prophets who have spoken have foretold these days. And you are heirs of the prophets and of the covenant God made with your fathers. He said to Abraham, 'Through your offspring all peoples on earth will be blessed.' When God raised up His servant, He sent him first to you to bless you by turning each of you from your wicked ways." (Acts 3:24–26)

In Acts 4, Peter and the other apostles encounter intense persecution. While they were still speaking at the Temple, the guards seized Peter and John and put them in jail. Even though their sermon was interrupted before they got to the altar call, so many people were persuaded by their message that the church swelled to more than five thousand people. Its rapid growth threatened the power of the religious leaders, so Peter and John were put on trial by the Sanhedrin, the same religious body that had plotted the death of Jesus.

But the apostles didn't defend themselves or plead for mercy. No, they preached the Gospel! The members of the Sanhedrin were furious, and they commanded the apostles to stop preaching about Jesus. Peter and John replied, "Which is right in God's eyes:

to listen to you, or to Him? You be the judges! As for us, we cannot help speaking about what we have seen and heard" (Acts 4:19–20).

Acts 6 and 7 record the martyrdom of Stephen—and the introduction of a young Pharisee and enemy of Christianity named Saul. Chapter 9 records Saul's miraculous conversion; he soon became known as the Apostle Paul, the greatest Christian missionary of all time. God used Paul and his companions (including Luke, the author of Acts) to rapidly expand the geographical borders of His Kingdom. Most of the rest of the book deals with Paul's missionary adventures.

In Acts 8:12, Philip the Evangelist proclaims "the good news of the kingdom of God and the name of Jesus Christ" and many who heard him "were baptized, both men and women."

In Acts 14, Paul and Barnabas preach the Gospel and win many disciples throughout southern Asia Minor (modern Turkey). They also faced harsh persecution there. As a result, they encouraged their disciples to remain true to their faith in Jesus. "We must go through many hardships to enter the kingdom of God," they said (Acts 14:22).

Later, Paul went to Ephesus in western Asia Minor, near the Aegean Sea. There, he remained for three months speaking daily in the synagogue and "arguing persuasively about the kingdom of God" (Acts 19:8).

Proclaiming the Kingdom with Boldness

In the final chapter of Acts, we see Paul under house arrest in Rome. After enduring years of religious persecution, he now faced Roman prosecution. Yet he refused to be silenced. Hundreds of Romans came to hear him preach. Luke says that they

came in even larger numbers to the place where he was
staying. He witnessed to them from morning till evening,
explaining about the kingdom of God, and from the Law
of Moses and from the Prophets he tried to persuade
them about Jesus. (Acts 28:23)

The final verse speaks of Paul's passion for inviting people into
the Kingdom of God: "He proclaimed the kingdom of God and
taught about the Lord Jesus Christ—with all boldness and without
hindrance!"

Here again, we see the amazing unity of the Word of God. The
message of the Kingdom of God began in Genesis. It was woven
throughout the books of the Law, the histories, the wisdom books,
and the Old Testament prophets. That message then springs forth
with a shout of triumph in the four gospels and the book of Acts.

The message of the Christian church is the proclamation of the
Kingdom of God, which all are invited to enter by grace through
faith in Jesus the Messiah.

18

The Epistles: One Church, One Covenant, One Kingdom

St. Paul's Chapel, built in 1766, is the oldest church building in New York City. George Washington visited and worshiped there.

The rear of the building faces Church Street, opposite the site of the World Trade Center. On September 11, 2001, when two hijacked airliners struck the twin towers, both collapsed. In all, nearly three thousand people died that day.

As the towers fell, debris rained down over St. Paul's Chapel. A thick layer of gray ash and concrete dust settled onto its roof and spire, filtering into the chapel interior as well as the streets.

Many buildings around Ground Zero were severely damaged—but St. Paul's was miraculously unharmed. There wasn't even a cracked window. Smoke and dust particles damaged the chapel's pipe organ, but after repairs and cleaning, it was as good as new.

One huge steel beam from the collapsed tower had been hurtling toward the chapel but was stopped by a giant sycamore tree on the northwest corner of the property. The tree was uprooted by the beam, but it protected the chapel from harm.

I think there's a symbolic message for us in this story. When our world is collapsing, crumbling to dust, and coming apart at the seams, where can we find the faith, strength, and encouragement to stand firm? We should go to the namesake of this chapel, to the letters of Paul and his fellow writers—Peter, John, Jude, and the writer to the Hebrews. They contain indispensable wisdom for understanding and living out the Christian faith.

The New Testament letters (or "epistles") also demonstrate the unity of God's Word, as well as the continuing themes of the Kingdom of God and the New Covenant. They show us that God's Kingdom is invisible—a spiritual manifestation at this present time. But a time is coming when the Kingdom will be visibly manifested, and the entire world will come under God's sovereign rule.

The Epistles of Paul

Paul wrote thirteen letters, which are some of the earliest books of the New Testament and make up about one-fourth of it. He wrote them largely to the fledgling churches he had founded in Asia Minor and Greece and to certain individuals. Many of them address specific problems that arose in the early church.

Three of them, known as the Pastoral Epistles, were addressed to two church leaders, Timothy and Titus. They contain guidance on how to structure and organize a church.

Four others, known as the Prison Epistles, were composed while Paul was in prison, awaiting trial in Rome. They were written between AD 60 and 62 and consist of Ephesians, Philippians, Colossians, and Philemon.

Here is an overview of their themes.

The book of Romans sets forth God's plan for salvation by grace through faith in Jesus Christ. In this book, Paul clearly presents the Gospel—and it is, of course, a Kingdom gospel. He wants to make it clear to his readers that one enters the Kingdom of God not by keeping religious rules and practices, but by having a faith relationship with Jesus Christ.

In Romans 14:17, he writes, "For the kingdom of God is not a matter of eating and drinking, but of righteousness, peace, and joy in the Holy Spirit." The "eating and drinking" he speaks of does not refer to having meals but to keeping the legalistic Jewish dietary customs and restrictions. Some people were teaching that, in order to be a Christian, a person had to believe in Jesus *and* keep all the Jewish laws and rituals. Paul made it clear that citizenship in the Kingdom is a matter of grace by faith in Jesus, period.

Paul outlines the essential Christian gospel in Romans: God's holiness, human sin, and the salvation offered through faith in Jesus. Paul's writing is thoughtful and clear. He grounds his New Covenant message in the bedrock of the Old Testament. For example, in Romans 11:26–27, he quotes from Isaiah and Jeremiah:

> As it is written: "The deliverer will come from Zion; he will turn godlessness away from Jacob. And this is my covenant with them when I take away their sins."

Paul wrote 1 Corinthians to correct a serious moral problem along with issues of conflict and disunity in the young church at Corinth. In 1 Corinthians 4:20, he said, "For the kingdom of God is not a matter of talk but of power." He was addressing a situation in which people claimed to have spiritual gifts, but their lives did not demonstrate the power of the Gospel. He wanted to remind them that life in the Kingdom requires love and obedience—the evidence of the life-changing power of the Holy Spirit working through believers.

In 1 Corinthians 11:25, Paul directly addresses the New Covenant in his instructions for the communion table, reminding his readers that Jesus took the cup and said, "This cup is the new covenant in My blood; do this, whenever you drink it, in remembrance of Me."

Paul wrote 2 Corinthians as a deeply personal defense of his apostleship. He also gave instructions for taking up collections for the poor in Jerusalem. The theme of the New Covenant emerges strongly in 2 Corinthians 2 and 3. Paul writes that God "has made us competent as ministers of a New Covenant—not of the letter but of the Spirit; for the letter kills, but the Spirit gives life" (2 Corinthians 3:6).

First-Class Citizens of the Kingdom

Some scholars believe Galatians may have been written as early as AD 48, which would make it the first of Paul's letters. In this book, Paul makes a powerful case that we do not enter the Kingdom of God by obeying the Law of Moses but through faith in Jesus Christ.

"But if you are led by the Spirit," he writes in Galatians 5:18, "you are not under the law." At the same time, a person who lives a lifestyle of sin does not have a saving faith. Paul goes on to say,

> The acts of the flesh are obvious: sexual immorality, impurity and debauchery; idolatry and witchcraft; hatred, discord, jealousy, fits of rage, selfish ambition, dissensions, factions and envy; drunkenness, orgies, and the like. I warn you, as I did before, that those who live like this will not inherit the kingdom of God. (Galatians 5:19–21)

Paul wrote Ephesians from prison. This book offers practical advice on how to live as a citizen of the Kingdom in a hostile and godless world. Paul makes it clear to the growing number of Gentile believers that they are first-class citizens of the Kingdom, equal to their Jewish brothers and sisters in every way.

He underscores the unity of the church by describing it as the "body of Christ." He says the God gave spiritual gifts "so that the body of Christ may be built up" (Ephesians 4:12). He reminds the readers, "No immoral, impure, or greedy person—such a person is an idolater—has any inheritance in the kingdom of Christ and of God" (Ephesians 5:5)—and he urges them to prepare for spiritual warfare by putting on the armor of God (Ephesians 6:10–17).

Philippians is one of Paul's most personal letters. It's clear from internal evidence that he wrote it from prison, probably his second and final imprisonment in Rome, prior to his execution. He speaks of his sense of approaching death, yet the letter is not dismal or depressing. In fact, Paul shares the secret of his contentment and his ability to rejoice in the Lord amid trials and hardships: he knows that his sufferings are helping to advance the Gospel.

Colossians is also a prison epistle. In the first section, the doctrinal section, Paul proclaims Jesus Christ to be the supreme Lord over the entire universe:

> For in him all things were created: things in heaven
> and on earth, visible and invisible, whether thrones or
> powers or rulers or authorities; all things have been cre-
> ated through him and for him. (Colossians 1:16)

He also tells us that God has "rescued us from the dominion of darkness and brought us into the kingdom of the Son he loves" (Colossians 1:13). Chapters 2 through 4 contain warnings against false teachers and set forth rules for Kingdom conduct.

Paul wrote 1 Thessalonians to the church at Thessalonica to encourage that young church to keep the faith and stand firm during a time of intense persecution. He probably wrote it between AD 49 and 51, making it one of his earliest letters. In it, Paul urges the Thessalonian believers to "live lives worthy of God, who calls you into His kingdom and glory" (1 Thessalonians 2:12).

Shortly after the first letter, probably around AD 51 or 52, Paul wrote a second letter to the Thessalonians to teach them sound doctrine about the end times, the Antichrist, and the second coming of Christ. He reminds them of their citizenship in the Kingdom, writing,

> We boast about your perseverance and faith in all the
> persecutions and trials you are enduring....As a result
> you will be counted worthy of the kingdom of God, for
> which you are suffering. (2 Thessalonians 1:4–5)

The Pastoral Epistles

Next, Paul wrote the Pastoral Epistles—two letters to Timothy, the bishop of Ephesus, and one letter to Titus, a missionary on the island of Crete. All three reflect the wisdom of an experienced missionary near the end of his ministry. They also reflect his deep concern for the next generation of missionary pastors who would continue the work after his death. The letters deal with church organization, the qualifications for elders and deacons, the danger of false teachers, and maintaining doctrinal purity.

The book of 1 Timothy includes instructions on the healthy functioning of a church and on guarding the truth from doctrinal errors.

Paul wrote 2 Timothy shortly before his death. It's a profoundly moving letter in which he refers to Timothy as his son. He urges Timothy to preach Christ boldly, not with timidity, and he asks him to visit and to bring Mark with him, saying, "For I am already being poured out like a drink offering, and the time for my departure is near" (2 Timothy 4:6). Along with a few greetings and brief instructions, Paul's final message to Timothy is,

> The Lord will rescue me from every evil attack and will bring me safely to His heavenly kingdom. To Him be glory for ever and ever. Amen. (2 Timothy 4:18)

Paul's letter to Titus deals with the qualifications and duties of elders and bishops. He also mentions Titus in Galatians 2:1–3 as a Gentile Christian missionary and one of his traveling companions in his early ministry. Titus helped establish the church on the island of Crete.

One of the shortest books in the Bible, Paul's letter to Philemon deals with Christian love, forgiveness, and reconciliation—all essential values of Kingdom living. In many of Paul's letters, he begins by asserting his authority as an apostle, but in Philemon, he appeals to the reader on a much humbler basis: "Paul, a prisoner of Christ Jesus." The underlying story is that Onesimus, a slave who ran away from his master Philemon, was returning with this letter in hand, seeking his mercy and forgiveness. Paul entreated Philemon to receive Onesimus not on the basis of a master receiving a slave, but on the basis of a Christian receiving a brother.

Hebrews: A Superior Covenant

The author of the letter to the Hebrews is unknown. Even so, some people claim it was written by Paul. Others have suggested Barnabas, Luke, Apollos, Priscilla, or Clement of Rome as the author. Whoever may have written it, Hebrews was accepted as Scripture because of its sound doctrine. Two major themes are the case for the divine nature of Jesus Christ, the Son of God; and the essential role of faith in the Christian life. Hebrews tells us that Jesus the Son is "the radiance of God's glory and the exact representation of His being, sustaining all things by His powerful word" (Hebrews 1:3). The theme of the Kingdom of God emerges in Hebrews, reminding us that

> since we are receiving a kingdom that cannot be shaken,
> let us be thankful, and so worship God acceptably with
> reverence and awe. (Hebrews 12:28)

The author makes it clear that the New Covenant established by Jesus is superior to the Old Covenant with Moses, arguing that the Covenant of Moses was a foreshadow of the good things to come in the New Covenant and was never intended to be the full and final revelation of God's grace:

> But in fact the ministry Jesus has received is as superior to theirs as the covenant of which He is mediator is superior to the old one, since the new covenant is established on better promises. For if there had been nothing wrong with that first covenant, no place would have been sought for another. (Hebrews 8:6–7)

The author also emphasizes the superiority of the New Covenant priesthood and sacrifice of Jesus over the Old Covenant priesthood and sacrifices. The Levitical priesthood established by the Law of Moses was inadequate because its priesthood was sinful and imperfect, in contrast to our sinless and perfect Great High Priest, Jesus. As Hebrews tells us, "Therefore, since we have a great high priest who has ascended into heaven, Jesus the Son of God, let us hold firmly to the faith we profess" (Hebrews 4:14).

The General Epistles

The General Epistles are the seven New Testament letters written by James, Peter, John, and Jude. Here again we see the unity of God's Word as these four writers present seven facets of a message that is consistent from Genesis to Revelation. It is a message of one Messiah, one Kingdom, and one New Covenant. These seven letters tell us how we ought to live as followers of Jesus, as citizens of the Kingdom, and as ministers of the New Covenant. Let's survey each letter.

James is filled with practical encouragement for Kingdom living, especially during a time of intense persecution. The author of the letter is James, the brother of Jesus, also known as James the Just. According to the historian Josephus in *Jewish Antiquities*, James was martyred in AD 62, so this letter was written in the 40s or 50s, making it one of the earliest-written books of the New Testament. James addresses the letter "To the twelve tribes scattered among the nations"—so the audience he has in mind is essentially Jewish Christians dispersed beyond the borders of Israel. He writes,

> Listen, my dear brothers and sisters: Has not God chosen those who are poor in the eyes of the world to be rich in faith and to inherit the kingdom He promised those who love Him? (James 2:5)

The key concept in James is patient endurance amid hardships and persecution. He writes:

> Consider it pure joy, my brothers and sisters, whenever you face trials of many kinds, because you know that the testing of your faith produces perseverance. Let perseverance finish its work so that you may be mature and complete, not lacking anything. (James 1:2–4)

Under the umbrella of this theme of patient endurance, James explores a series of subthemes: the importance of praying for wisdom, living humbly, controlling anger, tempering our speech, living a moral life, feeding on the Word of God, avoiding favoritism, living as peacemakers, and putting faith into action. By urging his readers to live by the values of the Kingdom, James shows us what the people of the New Covenant should look like.

Like James, the first letter of Peter offers encouragement to believers in a time of extreme suffering and persecution. Peter addresses his letter to "God's elect, exiles scattered throughout the provinces of Pontus, Galatia, Cappadocia, Asia, and Bithynia." At its close, he writes, "She who is in Babylon, chosen together with you, sends you her greetings" (1 Peter 5:13). "Babylon" probably refers to the city of Rome, and "she" probably refers to the church there. Peter writes tellingly of the persecution of that era:

> In all this you greatly rejoice, though now for a little while you may have had to suffer grief in all kinds of trials. These have come so that the proven genuineness of your faith—of greater worth than gold, which perishes even though refined by fire—may result in praise, glory and honor when Jesus Christ is revealed. (1 Peter 1:6–7)

Peter encourages his readers to live holy lives, to put away slander and deceit, to feed on the Word of God, to endure injustice and oppression without bitterness or retaliation, to dress modestly and live respectfully toward one another, and to maintain the unity of Christian love. Our motivation for living such lives, he says, is that as God's royal nation, we should live worthily of His calling upon our lives:

> But you are a chosen people, a royal priesthood, a holy nation, God's special possession, that you may declare the praises of Him who called you out of darkness into His wonderful light. (1 Peter 2:9)

In Peter's second letter, the great apostle who walked with Jesus delivers his final words to the Church. He probably wrote this letter between AD 65 and 68, shortly before he was martyred in Rome by Nero. Peter warns the Church against false teachers and encourages believers to press on in faith. He makes this appeal to live out the lifestyle of the Kingdom:

> For this very reason, make every effort to add to your faith goodness; and to goodness, knowledge; and to knowledge, self-control; and to self-control, perseverance; and to perseverance, godliness; and to godliness, mutual affection; and to mutual affection, love. For if you possess these qualities in increasing measure, they will keep you from being ineffective and unproductive in your knowledge of our Lord Jesus Christ. (2 Peter 1:5–8)

In this poignant letter, Peter says that Jesus has shown him that his death is near:

> I think it is right to refresh your memory as long as I live in the tent of this body, because I know that I will soon put it aside, as our Lord Jesus Christ has made clear to me. (2 Peter 1:13–14)

Peter makes numerous references to the Old Testament in this letter, plus a reference to the writings of "our dear brother Paul" (2 Peter 3:15). He urges his readers to eagerly anticipate "a rich welcome into the eternal kingdom of our Lord and Savior Jesus Christ" (2 Peter 1:11), and closes by encouraging them to look forward to the triumphant return of the Lord Jesus.

Evangelical scholars agree that the Apostle John wrote the Gospel of John, the three letters of John, and the book of Revelation. Read the opening lines of his gospel, then read the opening lines of

1 John and note the similarities. Both passages are written in lofty poetic language and describe Jesus as the Word (*Logos*) of God, the source of life and light. John's gospel begins, "In the beginning..." and 1 John begins, "That which was from the beginning ..."

In 1 John, the apostle states that he is an eyewitness of the life, death, and resurrection of Jesus, saying that everything

> which we have heard, which we have seen with our eyes,
> which we have looked at and our hands have touched—
> this we proclaim concerning the Word of life. (1 John 1:1)

This letter contains some of the Bible's most comforting descriptions of God's unfailing love as well as its most compelling exhortations to love God and love one another. Again and again, John emphasizes the importance of abiding in the truth. "If we claim to have fellowship with Him and yet walk in the darkness, we lie and do not live out the truth," he writes in 1 John 1:6. And in 1 John 3:18, he adds, "Dear children, let us not love with words or speech but with actions and in truth."

In 2 John, the apostle again urges believers to walk in the truth and in love, and warns them not to be deceived by false teachers. In verse 6 of this one-chapter letter, he writes, "And this is love: that we walk in obedience to His commands. As you have heard from the beginning, His command is that you walk in love."

In 3 John, the apostle addresses his "dear friend Gaius." Nothing is known about Gaius, other than what John says in this letter. Gaius is faithful to the truth, and he demonstrates love and kindness to fellow Christians and strangers. John asserts that showing hospitality to others is evidence of our love for God's truth. The values John writes of are Kingdom values.

John also writes about a man named Diotrephes, a prominent leader in the church who "loves to be first," and who uses his powerful position to oppose John's message and to spread "malicious nonsense" about him. Down through the ages, there have always been people like Diotrephes in the Church—people who love to be first, who crave attention and power, and who spread gossip in order to gain more power. Such people cause enormous damage to the Church and the Gospel, and they must be confronted, just as John, in verse 10, says he will confront Diotrephes.

Finally, John commends a believer named Demetrius who has an excellent reputation as a person who does good and obeys God.

The letter of Jude was written by Jude, also known as Thaddaeus, who was one of the twelve apostles (see Matthew 10:3 and Mark 3:18) and deals with the rise of false teachers in the early Church. Jude emphasizes contending for the faith, resisting false teaching, and encouraging those who struggle with doubt to come to a stronger faith.

Good Medicine for a Sick and Dying World

The world is sick and getting sicker every day. The sexual revolution keeps digging a deeper hole of depravity and dragging our children into it. Our government is more corrupt than ever before, and our news outlets hide our leaders' misdeeds. Couples readily break their marriage vows to pursue unbridled lusts. Globally, we see nation raging against nation; we see wars and hear rumors of wars.

Even in the Church of Jesus Christ, many preachers have abandoned the truth in order to win acceptance and popularity. Many who once had a strong biblical stance now question the authority of Scripture. False teachers and false gospels shout to us from all sides.

But God, in His Word, has given us a potent antidote to the spiritual sickness of this dying world. You find it in the New Testament letters of Paul, Peter, John, and the rest. In these letters you find good medicine for what ails this world—and what threatens the Church today.

We are surrounded by the kingdom of Satan and the corrupt kingdoms of this fallen world. We desperately need the Kingdom message of these New Testament letters. By meditating on these letters, we will continue to be healthy citizens of the Kingdom of God.

19

Revelation: God's Kingdom Promise Fulfilled

A theist philosophers and godless scientists tell us that life on Planet Earth is meaningless and doomed to despair. Carl Sagan once called our world

> a mote of dust suspended in a sunbeam.... Our planet is a lonely speck in the great enveloping cosmic dark. In our obscurity, in all this vastness, there is no hint that help will come from elsewhere to save us from ourselves.[1]

But praise God, the book of Revelation assures us that the atheists are wrong. God cares deeply about the future of Planet Earth—and He cares deeply about us. Revelation is God's guarantee that He has a plan to bring human history to a triumphant conclusion.

God's Word is a consistent whole because our God is a consistent God. Revelation is the finishing touch on God's masterpiece, the Bible.

The Kingdom of God Yesterday, Today, and Tomorrow

The Bible encompasses the entire history of the human race. In the beginning, Genesis tells the story of the creation and fall of humanity. At the end, Revelation reveals the eternal destiny of all believers.

In Revelation 1:19, the Lord Jesus tells John that He is going to reveal the past, the present, and the future. He says, "Write, therefore, what you have seen [*the past*], what is now [*the present*], and what will take place later [*the future*]." These three aspects of time are important concepts in God's Word.

The past, present, and future are essential aspects of our salvation. We *have been* saved and changed into new creations. We *are being* saved and changed through a process of sanctification. We *shall be* saved and profoundly changed at the resurrection of all believers, or the Second Coming of Jesus.

In the same way, the Kingdom of God exists in the past, the present, and the future. Two thousand years ago, Jesus announced, "The kingdom of God has come near" (Mark 1:15). Yet the Kingdom is currently present among us because God Himself reigns in our hearts. But it will come in its most dramatic and final sense when King Jesus returns in the future to establish it in all its glory and power.

There are other events in Revelation that have past, present, and future aspects. We think of the Great Tribulation as a *future* time of unimaginable calamity and persecution of the saints (as predicted in Daniel 7, Matthew 24, and Revelation 6 and 13). But it is also a *past* and *present* event. Christians in the first century were fed to the lions, crucified, or burned alive for Nero's cruel amusement. The Thessalonian church endured such bitter persecution that they feared they had entered the Tribulation and had missed the Lord's return (see 2 Thessalonians 2).

And today, thousands of Christians are martyred for their faith every year (estimates range from 7,000 to 100,000 annually, depending on surges of terrorism, revolutions, and religious tensions), yet their stories are seldom reported by the news networks. Ten years ago, a BBC reporter quoted one authority who said, "Two-thirds of the 2.3 billion Christians in the world today live…in dangerous neighborhoods. They are often poor. They often belong to ethnic, linguistic, and cultural minorities. And they are often at risk."[2]

For many Christian families in the world today, tribulation is a present-day reality.

The Apostle Who Received the Revelation

The book of Revelation opens with these words:

> The revelation from Jesus Christ, which God gave him to show His servants what must soon take place. He made it known by sending His angel to His servant John, who testifies to everything he saw—that is, the word of God and the testimony of Jesus Christ. (Revelation 1:1–2)

John wrote Revelation around AD 96, after all the other apostles had been martyred. John was in his early nineties when he experienced this vision. Before, he had been leading the church at Ephesus and encouraging the believers to stand firm against the Great Persecution. That time of persecution began when Domitian was crowned emperor of Rome and demanded that Roman subjects burn incense before statues of him and chant, "Our lord and god." John warned the Church not to bow to idols, but to worship only King Jesus.

For this reason, the Romans saw John as a dangerous subversive. The government exiled him to Patmos, an island in the Aegean Sea. People often picture John being cast ashore on a desert island without food or water, but that was not the case. Patmos was a thriving Roman military outpost with shops and farms. John was free to live in a house and roam the island, but he could not leave as long as Domitian ruled Rome.

In AD 96, Domitian was assassinated by members of his own court and John was allowed to return to Ephesus, where he lived for a few more years, teaching, preaching, and mentoring believers.

In his Revelation vision, John is given the honor of being taken into Heaven to be reunited with the resurrected and exalted Lord Jesus. The vision begins with a message from the Lord to seven churches, which can be summed up in a simple phrase: "Never compromise!" That is still the Lord's urgent message for us today: Stand firm for the uncompromised Gospel of the Kingdom.

Some people think of John's vision as a dream, but I don't believe it took place while he slept. The things he saw and heard were not symbolic impressions from his unconscious mind. In a state of full wakefulness and awareness, John had a real, personal encounter with the Lord Jesus Christ.

In Revelation 1:10, John describes the moment the vision began. He was not sleeping; he was praying and filled with the Spirit: "On the Lord's Day I was in the Spirit, and I heard behind me a loud voice like a trumpet." That loud voice, we soon learn, was the voice of Jesus—the Alpha and the Omega, the First and the Last, who was dead and is alive forevermore.

John saw reality. He saw and heard the Lord Jesus Christ.

The Purpose of the Revelation

Of all the books of the Bible, Revelation is the only one that promises a blessing to those who read it. This promise appears at both the beginning and the end of the book:

> Blessed is the one who reads aloud the words of this prophecy, and blessed are those who hear it and take to heart what is written in it, because the time is near. (Revelation 1:3)

> "Look, I am coming soon! Blessed is the one who keeps the words of the prophecy written in this scroll." (Revelation 22:7)

Revelation has two purposes. First, Jesus is sending specific messages through John to His churches in Asia Minor. Revelation 1 and 2 consist of seven letters to seven churches—letters of both commendation and rebuke. Second, Jesus gives us through John an outline of future events, couched in symbolism and imagery. This prophetic outline is not a precise schedule of events, but a general summation of God's agenda for human history.

When will these events happen? Only God the Father knows. Jesus could return for His Church at any moment, today or ten thousand years from now.

In Revelation 22:12, He says: "Look, I am coming soon! My reward is with me, and I will give to each person according to what they have done." Skeptics sometimes point to these words and say, "Jesus said He was coming soon, but two thousand years later there's still no sign of His return." But the skeptics need to hear the words of Peter:

> Above all, you must understand that in the last days
> scoffers will come, scoffing and following their own evil
> desires. They will say, "Where is this 'coming' He prom-
> ised? Ever since our ancestors died, everything goes on
> as it has since the beginning of creation...."
>
> But do not forget this one thing, dear friends: With
> the Lord a day is like a thousand years, and a thousand
> years are like a day. The Lord is not slow in keeping
> His promise, as some understand slowness. Instead He
> is patient with you, not wanting anyone to perish, but
> everyone to come to repentance.
>
> But the day of the Lord will come like a thief.
> (2 Peter 3:3–4, 8–10)

The skeptics' objections are already answered in God's Word.
As believers, we must always be ready to face the Lord.

One-World Government and the Kingdom of Satan

Revelation predicts the coming of a one-world government
under the dictatorship of a Satan-possessed man we know as the
Antichrist. For many decades, we have been witnessing a growing
movement toward this establishment.

On February 17, 1950, James Warburg, the chairman of the
Council on Foreign Relations and a former economic adviser to
President Franklin D. Roosevelt, told a United States Senate subcommittee, "We shall have world government, whether or not we
like it. The question is only whether world government will be
achieved by consent or by conquest."[3]

More recently, British journalist and politician Lord Christopher Monckton reported on the goals for the 2009 United Nations Climate Change Conference in Copenhagen:

> A world government is going to be created.... [Delegates discussed] setting up a global government so that they could shut down the West, shut down democracy, and bring freedom to an end worldwide.[4]

Microsoft founder and unabashed globalist Bill Gates said he was disappointed that the Copenhagen conference failed to establish a world government. In a 2015 interview with *Süddeutsche Zeitung*, Germany's national daily newspaper, he said,

> We have global problems.... We always have army divisions ready to fight a war. But what about fighting disease? How many doctors do we have? How many planes, tents, scientists? If there were such a thing as a world government, we would be better prepared [to fight disease outbreaks].[5]

Five years later, the World Health Organization (WHO) was coopted by Communist China, actually hindering an effective response to the COVID-19 pandemic, resulting in countless unnecessary deaths.[6] Its complicity with Beijing proves the folly of Gates's hopes for a one-world government: Any global government that emerges will be ruled by totalitarians, not humanitarians.

What the advocates for a global government never consider is how to make sure its dictator rules wisely and benevolently. A global government will inevitably become what John predicts:

> The beast [the Antichrist] was given a mouth to utter
> proud words and blasphemies and to exercise its
> authority for forty-two months. . . . And it was given
> authority over every tribe, people, language, and nation.
> (Revelation 13:5, 7)

Revelation 6:1–8:5 records the opening of the seven seals, symbolizing a time of global terror and slaughter. The first six unleash a series of disasters upon the planet: famine, war, economic calamity, persecution, and signs in the heavens. These disasters are the direct result of the global dictatorship of the Antichrist, who rules during the Great Tribulation.

The Antichrist's power comes from Satan himself; he will pour all his deceptive strength into this person, who will appear to be the most charming and persuasive human being in history. The Antichrist will convince the masses to worship the Dragon, who is Satan himself:

> People worshiped the dragon because he had given
> authority to the beast, and they also worshiped the beast
> and asked, "Who is like the beast? Who can wage war
> against it?" (Revelation 13:4)

Both Daniel and Jesus speak of the Antichrist as setting up an abomination in the Temple in Jerusalem. He will demand to be worshiped instead of God, and he will impose a reign of terror on the world.

As Jesus is the full expression of God the Father in human form, the Antichrist will be the expression of Satan in human form. Jesus is the Holy One of God, while the Antichrist is the lawless one of

Satan. Jesus is the Son of God, while the Antichrist is the son of perdition. Jesus is the Man of Sorrows, while the Antichrist is the man of sin. Jesus came as the Suffering Servant, while the Antichrist will demand to be served.

The Signs of the Times

We must understand that Revelation is no mere prophecy of future events. It is a message to be applied to our daily lives. It's about the present—your life and mine, right here, right now.

Increasingly, people within and outside the church are asking the same question: "Are we nearing the end of the world?" Both Christians and non-Christians are coming to the same conclusion: History seems to be approaching a dramatic climax. In Matthew 24 and 25, Jesus described the signs of the time of His approaching return.

First, there would be widespread deception: "Watch out that no one deceives you. For many will come in My name, claiming, 'I am the Messiah,' and will deceive many" (Matthew 24:4–5). Today, waves of false teachers are inflicting false, unbiblical "gospels" upon the Church—the prosperity gospel, the progressive gospel, the social gospel, the "love wins" gospel, and others—deceiving many. Some mutilate the Bible, rejecting Old Testament history or New Testament warnings about Hell or the exhortations to moral purity.

Second, Jesus said, "You will hear of wars and rumors of wars....Nation will rise against nation, and kingdom against kingdom" (Matthew 24:6–7). The world today is a roiling cauldron of political tension and conflict. The United States abandoned Afghanistan in August 2021, leaving a murderous Taliban emirate to rule that chaotic country. Russia invaded Ukraine in

February 2022, a senseless war that continues to rage after killing tens of thousands of Ukrainians and Russians. Civil wars rage in Yemen, Somalia, the Maghreb, Sudan, and other parts of Africa. The Islamic State threatens Syria and Iraq while Boko Haram threatens Nigeria. Iran continues its effort to acquire nuclear weapons while threatening Israel. Communist China continues to breathe threats against Taiwan while infiltrating and undermining the West.

The role of China in Bible prophecy cannot be underestimated. Though the word "China" does not appear in the Bible, Daniel 11:44 tells us that the Antichrist will be alarmed by "reports from the east" and go off to war. Revelation 9:16 describes the great final war, in which an army from the East, numbering "twice ten thousand times ten thousand" (two million) soldiers, crosses into the Holy Land. Currently, there is only one army that large in all the world: the People's Liberation Army of China, with 2.185 million soldiers in uniform.[7]

Third, Jesus said, "There will be famines and earthquakes in various places" (Matthew 24:7). There will be natural catastrophes of staggering proportions in many places all over the world. As this book was being written in early 2023, a series of incredibly powerful quakes shook Turkey and Syria, killing at least fifty thousand people and injuring many more. It would not surprise me to learn that this is one of the very quakes that Jesus foresaw.

Fourth, He said believers would be hated and martyred: "Then you will be handed over to be persecuted and put to death, and you will be hated by all nations because of Me" (Matthew 24:9). When the world hates us, that rage is not directed against us, but against

God. When you suffer persecution, count it a privilege to suffer for the sake of Jesus.

Fifth, Jesus said there would be apostasy—a great number of people falling away from the true biblical faith. As persecution intensifies, many will forsake Christ and join the unbelievers. Jesus said:

> "At that time many will turn away from the faith and will betray and hate each other, and many false prophets will appear and deceive many people. Because of the increase of wickedness, the love of most will grow cold, but the one who stands firm to the end will be saved." (Matthew 24:10–13)

The sixth sign of the time of His approaching return: The Gospel of the Kingdom will go to the ends of the earth. Jesus said, "And this gospel of the kingdom will be preached in the whole world as a testimony to all nations, and then the end will come" (Matthew 24:14). All around the world, under Communist dictatorships and Islamic regimes, in the most inaccessible corners of Africa, Asia, and South America, the Good News of the Kingdom is changing lives. A day will come when the Gospel will have been preached to every tribe and nation—and then the end will come.

"By His Blood"

Jesus could return at any moment. The signs seem to be aligning for His imminent appearance. I believe Satan is intensifying his persecution of Christians because he knows his time grows short.

He knows the Bible better than we do, and he is fully aware that Revelation 20:10 predicts his doom in the Lake of Fire. He is desperate to do as much harm and take as many souls with him as he can.

Many churches are uncomfortable with the teachings of Revelation. Neither the baby Jesus nor the crucified Jesus make any demands of us—but the risen and glorified King of Kings demands our all.

Revelation is an essential, irreplaceable book. Without it, our understanding of Jesus Christ and the Christian faith would be incomplete. The Old Testament presents Jesus as the promised Messiah. The gospels present Him as the Teacher, the Suffering Servant, and the Crucified and Risen Lord. At the beginning of the book of Acts, Jesus is the Ascended Lord, seated at the right hand of the Father. In the epistles, we see Him as our Lord and Savior. But it is in Revelation that we truly see Him glorified and magnified, King Jesus enthroned in His Kingdom.

In Genesis 3:15, God promises that a future offspring of Eve will crush the head of Satan. Without Revelation, we would have the *promise* of Satan's destruction but not the *fulfillment*. John, in Revelation 1:5–6, tells us,

> To Him who loves us and has freed us from our sins
> *by His blood*, and has made us to be a kingdom and
> priests to serve His God and Father—to Him be glory
> and power for ever and ever! Amen.

Note the phrase I emphasized: "by His blood." We sing hymns about the blood of Jesus. We consider His blood when we gather before the communion table.

But think about this: the Apostle John, who wrote those words, had *seen* the blood of Jesus with his own eyes. He stood at the cross and watched it flow from His hands, feet, and side. John did not have to *imagine* the blood of Jesus as we do. He *remembered* it. Till the end of his days, he could never blot that image from his mind.

And John's message to us is to remember that blood, because only it can save us. Only the blood of Jesus can cleanse us. Only the blood of Jesus can free us from sin, shame, guilt, and condemnation. Jesus bled to give us life.

Revelation Ends the Debate

Revelation reveals the past, the present, and the future. In the first chapter, we see Jesus arrayed in glorious light, robed in white and gold, with hair as white as wool, with blazing eyes and a voice like the sound of rushing waters. We see Him as the Alpha and the Omega, the Beginning and the End, the One who holds the keys of death and Hades.

Revelation solves the mystery that baffled the Old Testament prophets. Isaiah duly recorded the words the Holy Spirit gave him, though he couldn't fully understand their meaning. In Isaiah 9, he wrote about the mighty and victorious Messiah who would come as a triumphant King. He would be called "Wonderful Counselor, Mighty God, Everlasting Father, Prince of Peace," and He would reign forever "on David's throne and over his kingdom."

Yet Isaiah also wrote in chapter 53 about a Messiah who "took up our pain and bore our suffering," who was "pierced for our transgressions" and "crushed for our iniquities," who was "oppressed and afflicted, yet He did not open His mouth," and was "led like a lamb to the slaughter." The ancient Jewish prophets and scholars couldn't reconcile these two images of the Messiah. In fact, many were convinced they described two different Messiahs—one who would suffer and die, and another who would reign in power and majesty.

Today we understand that these two Messiahs are one and the same. In Revelation, we see Jesus the Suffering Servant has become Jesus the Ruling King—and here, at the end of human history, He has come into His Kingdom—the Kingdom of Heaven. The entire universe is filled with His glory.

Maranatha! Come, Lord Jesus!

PART VI

The Book That Heals

The Bible is a love letter from the King to His beloved. It places us on the operating table, takes out what is hurting and killing us, then sews us up again. The Bible is the Book that heals us. We need to read it as if our lives depend on it—because they do!

20

The Healing Word of God

Jack and Harry Cohn were brothers who left New York to cofound the Columbia Pictures Corporation in Hollywood. One day, Jack told Harry about an idea for a movie based on the Bible.

"What do you know about the Bible?" Harry said. "I'll bet you fifty dollars you don't even know the Lord's Prayer."

"The Lord's Prayer? Sure, I know it! 'Now I lay me down to sleep...'"

With a sigh, Harry handed fifty dollars to Jack. "How about that! I was sure you didn't know it!"[1]

I wonder how many churchgoing Christians are just as confused about God's Word as those two movie moguls. I wonder how many couldn't tell you anything about the sequence of events, the people, or the themes of the Bible. I wonder how many just take bits and pieces from the Bible to form a ramshackle, incoherent faith.

When God speaks in His Word, He reveals the truth about Himself. But at the same time, He also reveals the truth about us. The Bible is not just words on paper. These words have power in them. These words bear fruit, produce results, and change lives.

But how many of us read, study, and meditate on God's Word?

In 2020, the American Bible Society, in cooperation with the Barna Group, a California-based polling firm, surveyed more than five thousand American Christians, asking how often they read the Bible on their own, outside of church, and found that only 9 percent of Christians read the Bible every day. Another 3 percent said they read the Bible four or more times a week, and 9 percent said they read it once a week. Fully 34 percent admitted that they never read the Bible at all. Remember, all of these respondents identified as churchgoing Christians.[2]

Because God's Word is so powerful and life-changing, I feel compelled to challenge you with an idea you may find shocking—and convicting:

Your respect for God can be measured by your respect for His Word.

Don't misunderstand me. I'm not saying that the Bible is equal to God. We do not worship The Book. We worship the Lord Jesus Christ. But you cannot tell me that you truly love God if you never open His Word.

Think back to your early experiences of romantic love. If your beloved wrote you a letter, what would you do with it? Would you set it on a shelf to read when you have more time? Would you let it gather dust unread?

If you could do that with a letter from your beloved, then I would have to question your love for that person. Why? Because a letter from someone you truly, desperately love will draw you irresistibly to its pages. You will want to read it, then re-read it—over and over again. You'll want to study every turn of phrase to extract every nuance.

An unopened letter says you don't really want to hear from that person. And so does an unopened Bible.

A Sword and a Scalpel

If we say we love God, we need to demonstrate a love and respect for His Book. We need to ask God to fill us with a desire for His truth. We need to ask God to use His Word to change our lives, revive us, and fill us with an all-encompassing love for Him. This is how we should view the Bible:

> For the word of God is alive and active. Sharper than any double-edged sword, it penetrates even to dividing soul and spirit, joints and marrow; it judges the thoughts and attitudes of the heart. Nothing in all creation is hidden from God's sight. Everything is uncovered and laid bare before the eyes of him to whom we must give account. (Hebrews 4:12–13)

This is a statement of the life-altering power of the Bible. God's Word is alive and active—it's not just words on paper. It has power. It has the will of God behind it. The Bible produces results. It has the ability to lead you to salvation, as the Apostle Peter tells us:

> For you have been born again, not of perishable seed, but of imperishable, through the living and enduring word of God. (1 Peter 1:23)

When the Word of God acts, God acts. When the Word of God delivers, God delivers. When the Word of God heals, God heals.

The writer to the Hebrews uses a rather shocking metaphor, comparing the Bible to a double-edged sword that cuts deeply. He is saying that the Bible cuts you open and lays everything bare before God. We cannot hide from the probing, penetrating, steel-hard truth of His Word.

I suspect that if the writer to the Hebrews were composing this epistle today, he might have chosen a slightly different metaphor. Instead of a sword, he might have chosen a surgeon's scalpel. When your body needs surgery, a scalpel is your best friend. There are three ways that a scalpel is good for you in the same way that the Word of God blesses your life:

First, the Word stretches you out on the surgeon's table, so that the Great Physician can look inside you and find out what's wrong with you.

Second, it pierces through your outer shell and opens you up so that the Great Physician can cut out all the things that don't belong there.

Third, it sews you back up again and heals you completely.

Let's look at each of these healing dimensions of God's living, active Word.

1. The Bible Stretches You Out on the Surgeon's Table

One of God's Hebrew names is *Jehovah Rapha*, "The Lord our Healer." Jesus is our Great Physician, and God's Word has the power to open us up and surgically remove our spiritual cancers. But let's face it: no one looks forward to undergoing surgery. Perhaps that's why few Christians read the Bible. We know the Word is a scalpel, and we fear undergoing spiritual surgery. We don't want to get on God's operating table and have our sins and character flaws exposed to His gaze.

When a patient is opened up during surgery, everyone in the operating room must be extremely careful about keeping the surgical environment sterile. The instruments are sterilized. Everyone on the surgical team scrubs to the elbow, then puts on sterile gloves. The surgical site on the patient's body is sterilized. No microbe or bacterium can be permitted to invade the patient's body, or serious harm could result.

I believe that, in the spiritual realm, there are spiritual "microbes" and "bacteria" that seek to infect us and ruin the healing work of the Word of God. When we open the Bible, Satan and our own fallen flesh try to neutralize its impact on our lives. Satan and the flesh try to keep us out of God's Word, or to distract us as we read and meditate. Stray thoughts come into our minds, and we start thinking of some chore we need to do or someone we need to call. Sometimes we find we can't absorb anything we're reading. While studying God's Word, Satan may even attack us with doubts.

We need to sterilize our Bible reading environment. We need to pray that God would focus our minds, settle our thoughts, and open our understanding. We need to turn off all our distracting devices. We must make up our minds that our time in God's Word shall be sacred, and we won't let any spiritual "microbes" or "bacteria" infect us while we are on His operating table.

Before God stretches us out on His operating table, we are like the person who is walking around, feeling fine, completely unaware that a cancerous tumor is growing inside him. He goes in for a checkup, and the doctors do some lab work and take some X-rays. Then the report comes back: There is cancer, and it must be surgically removed.

In the same way, most of us are unaware of the moral and spiritual cancer within us. We compare ourselves to the people around us and we think, "I'm doing just fine. Compared to him, compared to her, I'm a pretty good Christian. I'm sure God grades on a curve, and I'm probably in the middle."

But when we read the Word of God and discover His absolute standard of morality and spirituality, suddenly we don't feel so good. We realize that we are desperately, morally, spiritually sick. We need surgery.

I can personally testify that there have been many times when I have sat down in the early hours of the morning with God's X-ray machine lying open in my lap. I start out feeling good about myself and my way of life. I have no problems, no sin issues, no broken relationships in my life—or so I assume. I ask the Spirit of God to open my heart to His Word and begin reading the Bible. Then... *Uh-oh!* A verse jumps out at me. I think, *God is speaking to me!* Through His Word, God reveals some sin in my life that I wasn't even aware of.

Other times, I may approach the Bible in a state of discouragement or exhaustion, and I'll discover a word of inspiration and encouragement. Again and again, I find that when I open God's Word, I discover exactly what I need, whether it's a rebuke or a message of encouragement.

The Word of God stretches us on God's operating table—and that is why we need it. Tragically, that is also why we avoid it.

2. The Bible Performs Surgery on You

Second, the Word of God cuts us open with surgical precision. This is what the writer to the Hebrews had in mind by writing that the Word is "sharper than any double-edged sword." For the word translated "sharper," the writer could have chosen the more common Greek word *koptō*, which means to cut, strike, or hack, possibly with repeated blows. But the writer carefully chose the much rarer Greek word *tomos*, which means to cut cleanly, decisively, and with precision, as a scalpel cuts.

When you go into surgery, you go with the confidence that your surgeon will not be hacking at you with a blunt sword, but will skillfully wield a scalpel. The surgeon's practiced hand will guide that scalpel to the exact area that needs to be penetrated in order to save your life.

What does the writer mean by saying that the Word of God "penetrates even to dividing soul and spirit, joints and marrow"? It means that the truth of the Bible reaches the deepest recesses of your being and invades every cell of your spiritual nature. There is no part of your being that God's Word does not expose to the light. It stops at nothing.

As you lie on the Great Physician's surgical table, He sees everything. No pretense or cover-up remains in any area of your life.

But there's more! The writer to the Hebrews says that the Bible "judges the thoughts and attitudes of the heart." It opens up our hidden motives and peers inside us. It reveals the *real* reasons we do and say the things we do. Again and again, during my quiet times with God's Word, the Holy Spirit has revealed to me some hidden motive or attitude. And I have had to cry out to God and say, "Lord, sanctify and purify my motives!"

One of my professors used to say, "Good publicity is okay as long as you don't inhale it." In other words, don't let the honors and praises puff up your pride. I've always been grateful that he taught me not to inhale any good press that comes my way.

Jeremiah 17:9 reminds us, "The heart is deceitful above all things and beyond cure. Who can understand it?" We are experts at self-deception. We are geniuses at rationalizing and deluding ourselves. We become so accustomed to making ourselves look good to others that we start believing our own hype.

But the Word of God burrows deep inside us, disarming our defense systems, shattering our delusions, and unlocking the secrets we keep hidden in the vaults of our souls. The Word sorts out reality from falsehood. What we cannot do, the Word of God does. Like a surgeon's scalpel, it cuts into us with precision and removes exactly what needs to be removed.

3. The Bible Sews You Up Again and Heals Completely

What if God cut into us and removed what needed to be removed—and simply stopped at that point? There you are, lying on the table, your innermost being exposed, the cancer removed—but He doesn't sew you back up again. That would be a disaster. But thanks be to God, He is our *Jehovah Rapha*, the Lord our Healer, and He always finishes what He starts. After He stretches us out, He cuts into us, and removes the diseased part of us, He sews us back up again. He doesn't cut into us to wound us, but to heal us. And as Philippians 1:6 reminds us, "He who began a good work in you will carry it on to completion until the day of Christ Jesus."

Because of our fallen nature, we tend to avoid anyone who "knows too much" about us—including God. We run away from Him because He not only knows all of our secrets, but wants to help us grow and change—and we resist growth and change. But always remember this: God knows everything there is to know about you—and He still loves you!

Our God is the God who heals us, restores us, fulfills us, blesses us, enriches us, strengthens us, and—yes!—forgives us. Once we understand that He wants to pour out more grace, and more grace, and more grace on our lives, we will welcome His surgery for our souls. We will eagerly run to His Word and ask Him to open us up, clean out our lives, and sew us back up again.

That is why Hebrew 4:16 tells us, "Let us then approach God's throne of grace with confidence, so that we may receive mercy and find grace to help us in our time of need." When the Word of God reigns supreme in our lives, when the love and mercy of God are daily experiences for us, then we will no longer avoid His presence or His Word. No, we will *run* to His throne of grace with confidence, eager to receive His healing forgiveness into our lives.

This Book is God's healing Word for your life—your eternal life. Read it as if your life depends on it. Live in it every day. Share its healing power with others.

Boldly proclaim the good news: The Kingdom of God is here!

Notes

Introduction: Sixty-Six Books, One Story

1. Justin Taylor, "What Is This Book?," The Gospel Coalition, October 15, 2018, https://www.thegospelcoalition.org/blogs/justin-taylor/what-is-this-book.

Chapter 1: The Life-Changing Book

1. Leonardo Blair, "Less Than Half of Practicing Christians Read Their Bible and the Rest of America Is Even Worse," *Christian Post*, November 4, 2016, https://www.christianpost.com/news/less-than-half-practicing-christians-read-their-bible-rest-of-america-even-worse.html.

2. John R. W. Stott, *Issues Facing Christians Today* (Grand Rapids: Zondervan, 2006), 85.

Chapter 2: Two Testaments, One God

1. Richard Dawkins, *The God Delusion* (New York: Houghton Mifflin, 2008), 51.

2. Ibid., 283.

3. *Holman Bible Dictionary*, s.v. "Mercy, Merciful," https://www.studylight.org/dictionaries/eng/hbd/m/mercy-merciful.html.

4. Alfred Edersheim, *The Life and Times of Jesus the Messiah*, vol. II (New York: Longmans, Green, and Co., 1907), 710.

5. Kelly Sadler, "George Soros-Backed District Attorneys Are Ruining America," *Washington Times*, November 23, 2021, https://www.washingtontimes.com/news/2021/nov/23/george-soros-backed-district-attorneys-are-ruining; Charles Stimson and Zack Smith, "'Progressive' Prosecutors Sabotage the Rule of Law, Raise Crime Rates, and Ignore Victims," The Heritage Foundation, October 29, 2020, https://www.heritage.org/crime-and-justice/report/progressive-prosecutors-sabotage-the-rule-law-raise-crime-rates-and-ignore.

6. Emma Tucker and Peter Nickeas, "The US Saw Significant Crime Rise across Major Cities in 2020. And It's Not Letting Up," CNN, April 3, 2021, https://www.cnn.com/2021/04/03/us/us-crime-rate-rise-2020/index.html.

7. A. W. Tozer, *The Attributes of God,* vol. I (Camp Hill, Pennsylvania: Christian Publications, Inc., 2003), 43–44, 77–78.

Chapter 3: Rightly Dividing the Word of Truth

1. "Menelik II" in *Bartlett's Book of Anecdotes*, eds. Clifton Fadiman and André Bernard (New York: Little, Brown and Company, 2000).

2. Charles Spurgeon, "The Word a Sword," Bible Bulletin Board, May 17, 1887, https://www.biblebb.com/files/spurgeon/2010.htm.

Chapter 4: One King, One Kingdom

1. Rosalind Goforth, *Goforth of China* (London: Marshall, Morgan and Scott, 1937), 46.
2. Ibid., 46–47.
3. Rosalind Goforth, *How I Know God Answers Prayer* (New York: Harper & Brothers, 1921), 8–9.

Chapter 6: David and Solomon: Foreshadowing God's Kingdom

1. John Ashcroft and Gary Thomas, *Lessons from a Father to His Son* (Nashville: Thomas Nelson, 1998), 195–203.
2. The Riverside Church, "Ugly Truths by Rev. Adriene Thorne | October 23, 2022," YouTube, October 23, 2022, https://www.youtube.com/watch?v=Pwty4KWP5Ys.

Chapter 8: Psalms: The Songbook of the Kingdom

1. Debbie White, "Under Attack: Christians Are the Most Persecuted Religious Group on Earth, Research Reveals," *The Sun*, April 23, 2019, https://www.thesun.co.uk/news/8920568/christians-most-persecuted-religious-group-on-earth-pew-research.

Chapter 9: Wisdom of the Kingdom: The Books of Solomon

1. Ruth Jackson, "Professor Rosalind Picard: 'I Used to Think Religious People Had Thrown Their Brains Out the Window,'"

PremierChristianity.com, May 25, 2021, https://www.premier
christianity.com/interviews/professor-rosalind-picard-i-used-to
-think-religious-people-had-thrown-their-brains-out-the-window
/4359.article.

2. Ibid.

3. Ray C. Stedman, *Adventuring through the Bible* (Grand Rapids:
Discovery House, 1997), 277.

4. Annie Besant, *Is the Bible Indictable?: Being an Enquiry Whether
the Bible Comes within the Ruling of the Lord Chief Justice as to
Obscene Literature* (London: Freethought Publishing Company,
1877), https://www.gutenberg.org/files/38273/38273-h/38273-h.htm.

Chapter 10: The Fall of Israel: Broken Covenant, Broken Kingdom

1. Paul Wallace, "Charles Colson Told the Following Story in
an..." Sermon Central, October 12, 2005, https://www
.sermoncentral.com/sermon-illustrations/22117/charles-colson
-told-the-following-story-in-an-by-paul-wallace.

Chapter 12: "Minor" Prophets, Major Impact

1. Grace EV Free, "Grace EV Free Live Stream Service at 9:00 AM
- Sunday, January 1, 2023" YouTube, January 1, 2023, https://
www.youtube.com/watch?v=xdz8Y75QxeU.

Chapter 13: Promises Kept: Prophecies of the Coming King

1. Lex Fridman, "Avi Loeb: Aliens, Black Holes, and the Mystery of
the Oumuamua | Lex Fridman Podcast #154," January 14, 2021,
https://www.youtube.com/watch?v=plcc6E-E1uU.

2. Alfred Edersheim, *The Life and Times of Jesus the Messiah,* vol. II (New York: Longmans, Green, and Co., 1907), 710.
3. Lee Strobel, *The Case for Christ* (Grand Rapids: Zondervan, 1998), 234–43.
4. Augustus Hopkins Strong, *Systematic Theology: Vol. 1—The Doctrine of God* (Woodstock, Ontario: Devoted Publishing, 2017), 114.

Chapter 14: The Suffering Servant and the Kingdom

1. Antonia Fraser, *Cromwell: The Lord Protector* (New York: Grove Press, 1973), 38.
2. William Fields, *The Scrapbook: Consisting of Tales and Anecdotes, Biographical, Historical, Patriotic, Moral, Religious, and Sentimental Pieces in Prose and Poetry* (Philadelphia: Lippincott, 1857), 540.

Chapter 15: The Gospels: Four Storytellers, One Story

1. Mary Fidelis, "Give Me Your Sins… ," Our Lady of Solitude Monastary, January 5, 2015, https://desertnuns.com/give-me-your-sins/; Pope Francis, "Apostolic Letter: Scripturae Sacrae Affectus of the Holy Father Francis on the Sixteen Hundredth Anniversary of the Death of Saint Jerome" (speech, Basilica of Saint John Lateran, Rome, September 30, 2020), Vatican.va, https://www.vatican.va/content/francesco/en/apost_letters/documents/papa-francesco-lettera-ap_20200930_scripturae-sacrae-affectus.html.

Chapter 16: The Parables: Pictures of the Kingdom

1. Martin Luther King Jr., "I've Been to the Mountaintop" (speech, Mason Temple, Memphis, Tennessee, April 3, 1968), American Rhetoric, https://www.americanrhetoric.com/speeches/mlkivebeentothemountaintop.htm.

Chapter 19: Revelation: God's Kingdom Promise Fulfilled

1. Carl Sagan, "A Pale Blue Dot" (1994), The Planetary Society, https://www.planetary.org/worlds/pale-blue-dot.

2. Ruth Alexander, "Are There Really 100,000 New Christian Martyrs Every Year?," BBC News, November 12, 2013, https://www.bbc.com/news/magazine-24864587.

3. "James Warburg before the Subcommittee on Revision of the United Nations Charter," (1950) United States Senate, https://en.wikisource.org/wiki/James_Warburg_before_the_Subcommittee_on_Revision_of_the_United_Nations_Charter.

4. William F. Jasper, "The United Nations: On the Brink of Becoming a World Government," The New American, October 11, 2012, http://www.thenewamerican.com/world-news/item/13126-the-united-nations-on-the-brink-of-becoming-a-world-government.

5. Michael von Bauchmüller and Stefan Braun, "Bill Gates im Interview: 'Den Täglichen Tod Nehmen Wir Nicht Wahr,'" Süddeutsche Zeitung, January 28, 2015, http://www.sueddeutsche.de/wirtschaft/bill-gates-im-interview-den-taeglichen-tod-nehmen-wir-nicht-wahr-1.2324164.

6. Hinnerk Feldwisch-Drentrup, "How WHO Became China's Coronavirus Accomplice," Foreign Policy, April 2, 2020, https://foreignpolicy.com/2020/04/02/china-coronavirus-who-health-soft-power.

7.   "Top 10 Largest Armies in the World 2023," Infos10.com, June 23, 2023, https://infos10.com/largest-armies-in-the-world/; "2021 China Military Strength," Global Fire Power, 2021, https://www.globalfirepower.com/country-military-strength-detail.php?country_id=china.

Chapter 20: The Healing Word of God

1.   "Cohn, Harry," *Bartlett's Book of Anecdotes*, eds. Clifton Fadiman and André Bernard (New York: Little, Brown and Company, 2000). Some dialogue altered for clarity.

2.   Heather Clark, "2020 'State of the Bible' Report Finds Few Americans Read Bible Daily," Christian News Network, July 24, 2020, https://christiannews.net/2020/07/24/2020-state-of-the-bible-report-finds-few-americans-read-bible-daily.

Biblical Encouragement for You—Anytime, Anywhere

Leading The Way with Dr. Michael Youssef is passionately proclaiming uncompromising Truth through every major form of media, empowering you to know and follow Christ. There are many FREE ways you can connect with Dr. Youssef's teachings:

- Thousands of sermons and articles online
- TV and radio programs worldwide
- Apps for your phone or tablet
- A monthly magazine, and more!

Learn more at LTW.org/Connect